MW01093068

SUBMERGED

into the Presence of God

Teresa Odden

ISBN 978-1-64140-412-9 (paperback)
ISBN 978-1-64140-413-6 (digital)

Christian Faith Publishing, Inc.
832 Park Avenue
Meadville, PA 16335
www.christianfaithpublishing.com

Printed in the United States of America

Sheila and Bethany, I can't think of the right words with which to express my thanks for always believing that I could—for your endless support and prayers to complete this work for the Lord.

Contents

Introduction

The initial intent of this book was to challenge the Christian community to start turning up the noise and make God the most newsworthy topic of the day. The church is too quiet when it comes to proclaiming the good news of the Gospel of Jesus Christ. The world can't hear a whisper.

This is still of importance, but the more I wrote, God began to slowly change me, which resulted in this book looking much differently than I originally intended. *What I didn't anticipate was that the woman who started this book isn't the same one who finished it.*

When people asked me what my book was about, they would typically follow up with another question: "How do I know when God is speaking?"

What is different in this book compared to most books you could read about living in the supernatural wonders of God is that I will take you into my "prayer closet." You will see how God guided and continues to guide me personally, specifically, and supernaturally. It is where I experienced miracles through dreams, visions, even visitation of angels. It is how he empowers me to know and walk as he wills.

This book and my words aren't intended to give you a five-step plan how to pray, when to pray, and what to pray. This book is about you seeing how God desires to speak to us regularly and spectacularly and tangibly. Yes, I said tangibly!

God began to "switch up" the way I had spent time in prayer and reading my Bible. What changed drastically for me was not self-taught but God-taught (see 1 John 2:27 about how God teaches us). God stirred within me a fresh way to worship. God transformed my thinking through worshipping anew.

My time with God and experiences cannot be duplicated for they are my own personal moments with him. God drew me to himself in a different way during my personal time of prayer, and it is this that I believe he wants me to share with you. It is where we discover the *more* of God.

But you can have your own unending, vibrant walk with God if you ask him. If you haven't looked to see God anew, then perhaps it is time you let God switch up how you spend time with him. The Bible tells us we can share in his glory, and when we do, we have but one thing to boast about—that is Living and Loving God!

The Christian community must be heard. "Don't let anyone intimidate or silence you. No matter what happens" (Acts 18:11, J. P. Phillips New Testament, Phillips).

My stories are not meant to turn attention away from the *love* of God with a focus entirely on the *manifestations* of the supernatural power of God. To see God as anything other than supernatural is perhaps why you don't hear or see God in all his fullness and don't see God working miraculously. God pierced my soul with an intensity to know his glory more so that others will also discover God in the fullness of his glory.

A Christian leader demanded Bilquis Sheikh, a Muslim background believer, to state whether she was charismatic or not. In her book, *I Dared to Call Him Father*, her response illustrates that when it comes to God—who is supernatural—we cannot define him anymore than we can define who we are in him.

Having been posed the question, she picked up a quarter.

"Well, Father, you decide … heads, I'm Charismatic; tails, I'm not."

The silver coin spun blithely in the air, then dropped to her carpet. She could scarcely believe what she saw. Kneeling down to make certain, she chuckled. What better proof could she have of the Lord's sense of humor? The quarter had landed on the edge in the thick folds and was standing straight up. The lesson, Bilquis says, is that the important thing is not how we worship or what words we use or what tags we tie on. But do we love our neighbor? Are we guided by his Holy Spirit? Do we obey him implicitly? Do we weep for those who do not know Christ? Do we long to share our knowledge of him" (Sheikh, B. and Schneider, R. H., 1978, p. 11–12)?

I have shared numerous verses in the following pages—too many some may say. However, how often have we, as believers, taken no time to read the Bible and see the great treasury of God's love and promises for ourselves? The importance of knowing the Word of God to see how he speaks clearly and specifically from the Word cannot be overstated.

Many times, when I read Christian resources, I quickly skim the Scriptures because they are familiar. Instead, I jump over verses and begin absorbing the words the author has sown together. I ask you to ponder the Scriptures in the following pages and let *my* words be secondary to God's *perfect Word*, which guides into all Truth. Recognize how God's Word is alive and speaks directly into a specific situation or simply a confirmation of what we feel is going on inside our minds and our souls.

There are no substitutes to knowing God more and to devouring his Word, the Bread of Life. The more time I spend absorbing the Word of God, the more dissatisfied I am with a few verses and a five-minute prayer. It is from this desire that I see more of his glory and how he operators in the natural supernaturally.

---

*THERE ARE NO SUBSTITUTES TO KNOWING GOD MORE
AND TO DEVOURING HIS WORD, THE BREAD OF LIFE*

May his promises contained in the Bible become your promises and your purpose. I pray that you will look to the greatness of our God in ways too often left ignored. Together, may we experience his boundless creativity as Creator of all heaven and earth. Make God your "headline news."

"Sing to God, everyone and everything! Get out his salvation news every day! Publish his glory among the godless nations, his wonders to all races and religions. And why? Because God is great—well worth praising!... Splendor and majesty flow out of him, strength and joy fill his place. Shout Bravo! to God, families of the peoples, in awe of the Glory, in awe of the Strength: Bravo! Shout Bravo! to his famous Name" (I Chron. 16:23–36, MSG).

Part 1

Love of the Cross

1

Love of the Cross Vision

"Let me tell about the visions and revelations I receive from the Lord"
(2 Cor. 12:1, New Living Translation).

The most pleasant part of my days are in the morning when I sit at my kitchen table with a cup of coffee, Bible open, enjoying time with God. I don't use the word *enjoy* lightly. The definition of *enjoy* means to "like, love, be fond of, be entertained by, take pleasure in, be keen on, delight in, appreciate, relish, revel in, adore, lap up, savor, luxuriate in, bask in (Dictionary.com, 2015). This actually describes my expectations when I take time to talk to God and read my Bible.

I love to read a good novel, one that's difficult to put down. I try to anticipate what's next. I pick it up with excitement until I reach the end. Sometimes the story is predictable and sometimes not. If the story isn't predictable, it doesn't mean I like it any less. However, more often, it is the unpredictable book I enjoy most.

Books not only increase knowledge, but they also take me to unfamiliar places and evoke different emotions. Every time I open my Bible, I do so with the same excitement and with an expectation that I will learn more of God's character.

It is thrilling to know God will take me to unfamiliar places, and with him, I experience some of the most thrilling times of my life. Therefore, I am purposeful to have an attitude expectant for God to surprise me.

The Bible is where I go to know him personally and to anticipate something new in my life. When I go to God with excitement, "that fullness comes together ... his power extends" over every area of my life" (Col. 2:10, Amplified Bible).

Ephesians 3:19 beautifully describes God's promise that we can walk in his glory: "... The extravagant dimensions of Christ's love. Reach out and experience the breadth! Test its length! Plumb the depths! Rise to the heights! Live full lives, full in the fullness of God" (MSG). What a promise!

The more I plunged into his Word, the more my hunger increased to spend time with God. My time with God grew with a fresh and renewed sense of his extravagant goodness and generosity. Over time, he revealed himself in unpredictable ways, different from times past. One major difference was that I listened more intently and moved to action more quickly when God said to do something different.

I know that God is present everywhere at all times, but I also know there is a real and tangible presence of God that all believers can experience. In the Scriptures, God makes his presence known to his people in numerous and extraordinary ways. God's character never changes, and his being is limitless. He has no boundaries and is inexhaustible in every way. God is never bound by human thinking.

The first record we have of God's presence being felt was in the Garden of Eden. "Then the man and his wife heard the sound of the Lord as he was walking in the garden in the cool of the day" (Gen. 3:8, New International Version). I understand this to mean in that moment, they didn't hear his voice, but they heard his presence. I understand this to mean that the first encounter with God after sin was the sense of his presence approaching and then the sound of his voice.

What a wonderful gift of comfort and love and grace to let us experience God in our midst. I love how God wants to do the same for me and for you. For all those longing to see and feel his great beauty, it is not necessary to *feel* God's presence in order to trust his promise of his presence to be with us. But, oh, to feel him and his tangible loving presence! However, I don't want to limit God's desire to recognize him through his tangible, loving presence.

God continues to show me the way to recognize his tangible presence comes by cultivating an atmosphere of worship. *Worship instills an attitude to remove distractions of what is important to me and to focus on what is important to God.* Worship allows God to clear my mind, so I, too, can experience what Adam and Eve did and to "hear God walking" and to hear God speaking.

Because God is real and ever-present, there is a certainty he will speak. I can hear him, and I did. I was sitting quietly one morning, reading my Bible, waiting for a fresh word from God to start my day. It was then he descended from heaven to my heart in an unexpected way. He made his presence known to me out of a time simply devoted to prayer and a heart to worship and praise him.

I often ask God to pour over me, and he did that day. It was a morning unlike any I had experienced when God stepped in, and my senses were heightened to his overwhelming presence. The Spirit of God rested over me with such power I had to physically rest my head on the table. Biblically, it is similar to Paul's experience on the road to Damascus when a light suddenly appeared from heaven, and "he fell to the ground …" (Acts 9:3–4, New King James Version).

As I waited in silence, eyes closed, giving God permission to possess all my senses—every thought and action—God began imparting an illustration. Soon, a picture appeared from the darkness.

An image came before me of Jesus on the Cross. I spoke no words, but my heart was giving thanks for the sacrifice Christ made. My eyes *drifted* first to the base of the cross.

I could see his nail-pierced feet where the dirt was imbedded between his toes, dragging his weary feet through the stony, unpaved streets. His legs, knees, thighs barely visible from the amount of blood flowing out of the gashes from the brutal flogging. Every drop and stream of blood oozing where skin had been pulled apart. These were no surface skin abrasions but wounds cutting deep into his flesh.

It was hard to comprehend how a main artery had not been severed due to the amount of blood pouring from the ripped flesh he endured before he was nailed to the cross. Had an artery been severed, Christ's blood would have drained within a few moments, ending his life sooner rather than later. Instead, he lingered and endured the painful journey down the road of suffering, only to struggle up the hill to endure even greater agony of being nailed to and hanging on a cross while still alive. He survived each beating to walk the lonely road, fueled only by the love for mankind, for me.

I sensed not only the bruising of his body but, most of all, the bruising of his heart from the ridicule and public humiliation. Gradually, my eyes gazed upward where blood continued draining from his pierced side. As I looked upon him, I caught sight of his heavy breathing, a shortness of breath, skin covered in blood. *Jesus, thank you for enduring this pain, all the suffering for all humanity.*

It seemed no matter where I looked, there wasn't a piece of skin that was unscathed from the lashing that ripped through his flesh. The image was so horrific I wanted to look away, but my eyes remained fixated on him because I knew all he was enduring was for me. I could not get beyond "thank you." Thank you for carrying all my burdens, thank you for carrying my shame, and thank you for suffering what I should have suffered instead.

He was bruised, bleeding yet showed no reluctance to be scourged with instruments of torture so I could be protected and healed. There was no hesitation, only a willingness to endure unimaginable humiliation where all dignity was stripped away.

The *Love of the Cross* vision was how God began to open my heart to recognize more of his presence and to see him in ways I'd never experienced before. He was taking me back to the central focus of Christianity and why I follow Christ. It's what Andrew Murray describes as heavenly humility "that made Jesus on the throne willing to say, 'I will go down to be a servant, and to die for man … Jesus brought humility from heaven to us. It was humility that brought him to earth, or he never would have come" (Murray, 1953).

Most often, when I think of the cross, I focus on the motive of my heart, but Jesus was revealing the motive of his heart. Not only was I seeing what he had personally gone through for me, he was also sharing his feelings, his desires. I had the sense his heart was saying, "It's okay, I want to do this."

"Lord, I cannot comprehend this weight of heaviness you felt, because it wasn't just for me, it was for everyone (past, present, and future). My sin alone was painful enough. Thank you," I prayed. Yet I understood he was able to compartmentalize my sins from all others. Unlike humans who have to switch from task to task, thought to thought, God's omnipotent quality assures me he is thinking of me as a unique individual and all humanity simultaneously.

God's divine power is so tender, his humility so personal, his love without borders, and all display the majestic God of heaven.

Jesus was physically bound with chains, but his love has no boundaries. The world may want to create labels for what we've done, who we are, our race, ethnicity, but not God. God's love and forgiveness and grace has no limits.

> "Hosea put it well: I'll call nobodies and make them somebodies; I'll call the unloved and make them beloved. In the place where they yelled out, 'You're nobody!' they're calling you, 'God's living children'" (Rom. 9:20–33, MSG).

My eyes slowly made their way to the face of Jesus. Though I don't know what he looked like and my image was probably more from movies and paintings, I still grasped the image of the face of Jesus. Even if I knew what Christ looked like, he was so disfigured the Bible states he was beyond recognition (Isa. 52:14).

I could see his tears, tears of blood, slowly and steadily dripping down his cheeks. Soon, tears began to fall down mine. There were no words, only my heart—again saying, "Thank you."

Tears continued to cascade down my cheeks as I saw the crown of thorns with the sharp ends pierced into his head. I have seen the Queen of England's brilliant crown and scepter, adorned with one of the largest diamonds in the world. Here, there was no display of splendor or glory. The crown of thorns was not a prick or two from a needle, but an instrument of torture.

Jesus suffered with the absence of God's presence in his greatest hour of need. "My God, my God, why have you abandoned me?" (Matt. 27:46, MSG). It was this absence of the Father I cannot imagine having to bear. Many times in my life I have felt alone, but God was and is always with me. Christ could not say the same. He gave me a glimpse of his pain but, more importantly, the joy that came from his sacrifice.

Christ exercised his free will with an act of humility when he endured unimaginable torture and humiliation. He fulfilled what he was created to do because the immensity of his love is vast, and he knew the outcome. It was as though, simultaneously, he was able to endure while never losing site of the joy to come.

His suffering allows me to also not focus entirely on his suffering and my suffering but to see the hope and love that came by Christ hanging on the cross. Though the world at the time saw horror and disgrace, I was able to see a glimpse of the beauty and splendor of the Cross.

There was a consciousness that if I had not been prepared to worship, I would have been compelled to do so. A Scripture came to life that states, "Yet it was because of this that God raised him up to the heights of heaven and gave him a name which is above every other name, that at the name of Jesus *every knee shall bow* in heaven and on earth and under the earth, and *every* tongue shall confess that Jesus Christ is Lord, to the glory of God the Father" (Phil. 2:9–11, The Living Bible).

People from all walks of life and religions will automatically bow before the Lord God Almighty and worship him. There will be no hesitation and questioning who he is. They will know in the same way I saw him in my vision. Romans 14:11 states, "'As surely as I live,' says the Lord, 'every knee will bend to me, and every tongue will declare allegiance to God'" (NLT).

This will be the most wonderful day in history all because Jesus executed his free will out of love for me, for you. Thankfully, I have the gift of free will. I can choose to see God now by recognizing who he is.

A new and wonderful picture of what Christ did for me was how God began to instill a greater excitement and joy for passionate worship. I can write the story of my life, but God wants me to write the story of him in my life in an entirely new way.

> *"He had no beauty or majesty to attract us to him, nothing*
> *in his appearance that we should desire him.*
> *He was despised and rejected by mankind, a man*
> *of suffering, and familiar with pain.*
> *Like one from whom people hide their faces*
> *he was despised, and we held him in low esteem.*
> *Surely he took up our pain and bore our suffering,*
> *yet we considered him punished by God, stricken by him, and afflicted.*
> *But he was pierced for our transgressions, he*
> *was crushed for our iniquities;*
> *the punishment that brought us peace was on*
> *him, and by his wounds we are healed.*
> *We all, like sheep, have gone astray, each of us has turned to our*
> *own way; and the Lord has laid on him the iniquity of us all.*
> *He was oppressed and afflicted, yet he did not open his mouth;*
> *He was led like a lamb to the slaughter, and as a sheep before its*
> *shearers is silent, so he did not open his mouth … Yet it was the*
> *Lord's will to crush him and cause him to suffer, and though the*
> *Lord makes his life an offering for sin, he will see his offspring*
> *and prolong his days, and the will of the Lord will prosper in his*
> *hand. After he has suffered, he will see the light of life and be*
> *satisfied; by his knowledge my righteous servant will justify many,*
> *and he will bear their iniquities"* (Isa. 53:2–7, 10–11, NIV).

I was determined to not let go of this image, and the more I considered what Jesus did for me, I questioned how much of my own dignity I would be willing to give up for Christ. It is beyond my imagination to understand the spiritual strength needed to endure such suffering and pain and the willingness to do so. God did not stop with this vision that morning.

"Your love, God, is my song, and I'll sing it! I'm forever telling everyone how faithful you are. I'll never quit telling the story of your love— how you built the cosmos and guaranteed everything in it. Your love has always been our lives' foundation ..." (Ps. 89:1–3, MSG).

When the vision vanished, I was so overcome in God's presence. He invaded my heart, mind, body, and soul with an unexplainable stillness. God's presence was strong, and my sense of thought was focused entirely on God. Surrounded by God's beautiful stillness, he reminded me of two dreams I had previously.

At the time, I didn't realize it would be the first in a sequence of visions and dreams, illustrating the *how* to boast in what God has done for me and all mankind, to first look upon God from Christ's ultimate gift of love and how his love is beyond words.

I saw a picture of how sin can look and what it means for God to remove all sin. The timing was not a coincidence, and it seemed to indicate another chapter in God's story for me personally.

Until we understand what the cross represents to us personally and we grasp the full meaning of what Christ did for us, it limits our appreciation of God's love and his divine nature. Without faith, it's impossible to please God; faith begins with receiving the message of the cross.

Shortly thereafter, two dreams followed. God's story became my story. God spoke in a way that resonated to me personally, and it's what I call *Redeemed from the Inside Out Dreams*.

Redeemed from the Inside-Out Dreams

There were several snakes around me, and I was able to ward them off by tying them together ... Once they were tied up, they were no longer a threat and able to come at me. It's all I remembered, and I woke up feeling refreshed because I knew the enemy could not touch or harm me.

In a second dream that morning, I saw a picture of my legs. They were covered with boils and holes where green puss was oozing. I made a comment that it looked like a volcano, with puss erupting from the inside out and the disease being forced to the surface. As the puss erupted and pushed its way up and out, my pores were enlarged, creating a hole. Soon the puss disappeared, holes closed, and my legs were entirely covered in blood. I was disease free. My legs were completely healed.

End of Dreams

Interpretation of Redeemed from the Inside-Out Dreams

I woke up with these disturbing images. It is necessary to see how the Word of God aligns with a dream and message that I sense he wants me to pay attention to. Therefore, I could see how snakes represented the devil who tries to cause fear, and yet God revealed a beautiful illustration from these dreams of how the enemy has no control over my life.

The second dream revealed the result of what Christ did for us after hanging on the cross and how the blood of Jesus *pushes* sin and diseases from the inside out of our lives. It was similar to a skin abscess, an infection that doesn't belong in the body. An abscess must be dealt with or serious health complications can take place.

It is recommended to avoid touching and trying to push the puss out or the infection could spread. There are medications and treatments so the abscess will drain on its own, making its way to the surface of the skin and out of the body.

Just like an infection in the body can cause serious harm, so does the sin in our lives. We are unable to extract the sin on our own; it must be done God's way, and that's to simply acknowledge what he did on the cross and allow him to take what is within and extract it so we can have spiritual healing.

By his wounds and blood, we are forgiven and healed when we acknowledge and accept who he is and what he did for us (Isa. 53:5–6). Sin has no power over us. We are not bound by what we've done, but we can be free by who we are in Christ Jesus.

I had confidence any disease and sin was gone. Not only was it gone, but there was no residue. Instead, there was a beautiful sense of God's marvelous cleansing because he willingly accepted his death on the cross. It was as if I was seeing a fresh transfusion from the blood of Christ, cleansing my inner being, purifying my heart, mind, body, and soul.

God presented me with a beautiful and explicit account of his story and the process by which I need to focus on and believe in for total restoration. The necessity that his story must be my story and when I share my story, God creates a new narrative in my life that others can experience for themselves. They can choose to share in God's story of total healing from sin and disease, and that is where our stories of a changed life begin.

Through these dreams and visions, God was pointing me back to the simplicity of the gospel. It's no small thing; it's everything. They are what I call my God-stories.

It was then God reminded me of a phrase planted in my spirit many years ago: "Jesus wet the nails." More than two decades prior, God impressed this phrase on me, but I did not understand the significance of this simple phrase. Annually I would ask God what it meant. Before I ever began writing or realized writing was part of God's plan for me, I wondered if it would be the title of a book. I started a document with this phrase as a possible title, though it remained blank for decades. God wouldn't give me a phrase if it weren't for a specific purpose or understanding. Years later, this phrase has meaning.

In the Old Testament, the blood sacrifice was sprinkled over everything in the tabernacle and then on the people. Hebrews 9:20–22 describes the sacrifice: "This blood confirms the covenant God has made with you. And in the same way, he (the priest) sprinkled blood on the Tabernacle and *on everything* used for worship. In fact, according to the Law of Moses, *nearly everything was purified with blood.* For without the shedding of blood, there is no forgiveness of sins" (English Standard Version).

It was the blood sacrifice of animals that cleansed the people from their sins, until Jesus became the blood sacrifice. The blood that poured over my disease and sickness in this dream helps me carefully ponder what Jesus did for me personally. The blood that drained from his torn and open flesh, and over the nails, is what brings healing to me spiritually and physically.

Over two decades had passed after receiving these four simple words (Jesus wet the nails) as I stood in the back row during a Sunday evening service. God was expanding my appreciation of what he did for me. It's Christ's blood that covers all my sin. His blood was enough for every sin for every person. Why? Because he is perfect. So I never have to be! The blood is cleansing, redeeming, healing. His blood covers all sins and as the lyrics to this old hymn from the 1800s illustrates so well:

"What can wash away my sins? Nothing but the blood of Jesus. What can make me whole again? Nothing but the blood of Jesus. Oh, precious is that flow, that makes me white as snow. No other fount' I know, nothing but the blood of Jesus" (Lowry, 1876, Hymnal 307).

This beautifully describes how God shifted my focus from me to him. God was taking me back to the central aspect of knowing him with a greater understanding of the significance of the cross.

"Perhaps now is the time to keep writing and see how God uses this title. I think it has so much power in the title of what he really did—the nails pierced his body and his suffering pierces my heart to come as I am. The blood of Jesus means more to me than ever," I journaled.

Then you can tell the next generation detail by detail the story of God, Our God forever, who guides us till the end of time" (Ps. 48:13–14, MSG).

My praise continued that morning and here is what I wrote in my journal when this time came to a close. "I praise you for …" And I couldn't stop listing everything he means to me and "because there is no end to his glory." "The Lord is pleased. His will be done on earth as it is in heaven. Sickness, disease, infirmities (generational). He is my hope. I'm in his care. My mind is empty except to say, 'I'm in Christ,' his presence invading my spirit. Praise the name of the Lord. No words can describe time in his presence this morning. Nothing. I hope I can remember this beautiful morning sitting, standing, bowing in his presence."

I believe one of the reasons God gave me such a strong experience of his presence was because of my determination to focus, to wait, and to listen. By doing so, God peaked my spiritual ears, which are often in the heart and mind. God disrupted my prayers that morning to show me the cross was not dry. It was necessary for the cross to be covered with the blood sacrifice of Jesus Christ in order for total cleansing and healing. At the end of my thanks, I could see how the *Love of the Cross* is revealed in four simple words.

"Jesus wet the nails."

2

Behind the Veil of Humility:
Power in Silence

"From the time the world was created, people have seen the earth and sky and all that God made. They can clearly see his invisible qualities–his eternal power and divine nature. So they have no excuse whatsoever for not knowing God" (Rom. 1:20, NLT).

I have been asked many times, "How do you know when God is speaking? How can I hear him as clearly as you do?" The key to knowing that it is God who speaks to you is recognizing God speaks supernaturally in the natural realm. Most often he speaks through his Word. Let me say that again because there is something in us that resist this. Most often he speaks through his Word. A reason he has continually reminded me to *love his Word* with all I've got. Without the Word feeding into my spirit, silence is what I experience most often.

The word *supernatural* means "attributed to some force beyond scientific understanding or the laws of nature" (Dictionary.com, 2015). The *force* that is beyond understanding is that of the Holy Spirit. I must listen to hear and be desperate to hear. This must be high on your list of priorities if you claim that it is important to you.

I can know for certain he will speak even though I don't know the manner in which he will do it.

At the risk of sounding redundant, I want to say to you again, most often, the way God speaks is through his Word. Therefore, every single time we read a passage in the Bible, God is speaking. The problem is people limit the intake of reading the Bible and I believe this is a major reason why people keep questioning if God is speaking.

When you keep waiting for an answer from God, don't neglect reading the Living Word. The Word of God breathes life into us and our situations. When we neglect the Word, we neglect God, and it can result in our not paying attention to him.

The verse 2 Timothy 3:16–17 states in The Message that "Every part of Scripture is God-breathed and useful one way or another—showing us truth, exposing our rebellion, correcting our mistakes, training us to live God's way. Through the Word we are put together and shaped up for the tasks God has for us."

Another way I have learned to recognize God speaking is through a sudden, quickening in my spirit. Suddenly the Holy Spirit steps in and there is a heightened sense something in the spiritual realm is taking place. It's where God consumes the center of my soul, which opens the doors of my heart to experience him more.

What happened on that beautiful morning when I saw the *Love of the Cross Vision,* God did again. Having few experiences with God, I believe, limits my knowledge of who God is. God wants to enlarge my awareness of him.

If I believe God created the world, why would I dismiss a conversation with him? I pause; I anticipate and expect that he will make his message known to me. This is not the time to dull my senses, but to remain alert while sitting in God's presence. It is a time for listening with my soul. To dull my senses would be to dismiss his presence and reject one of the greatest gifts we have—a personal and intimate friendship with God.

Most often when I question if God is trying to say something and I don't know it's him, it's simply because I'm not listening to hear. In the natural it is difficult to explain, however, an active prayer life and time devoted in God's presence is what it means to walk with the Holy Spirit.

It is in these moments the supernatural presence of God is made known to us. There can be a continuous flow of God's voice, but again, it's not in questioning, it's expecting God to speak in the natural realm and his supernatural being is what brings revelation into our souls.

For those who have encountered God's presence in a tangible way, you understand what I'm trying to say. For those who haven't, it is difficult to comprehend, but God manifesting himself is his desire for all of us. God doesn't operate by human thinking where we look for what is rationale. God operates beyond that which our minds can conjure up.

The Bible states in 1 Corinthians 2:14, "But people who aren't spiritual can't receive these truths from God's Spirit. It all sounds foolish to them and they can't understand it, for only those who are spiritual can understand what the Spirit means" (NLT). We can choose to believe and expect the unexpected.

God is my constant companion, and I love drawing close to his heart through prayer and reading the Bible. I want to submerge myself into the presence of God and reading his Word gives me the assurance he is present.

In Isaiah God's Word tells us that if we seek him, we can find him. God does not keep himself disguised and he is both intimately knowable (Isa. 45:19) and unsearchable (beyond human comprehension). "My thoughts are nothing like your thoughts," says the Lord. And my ways are far beyond anything you could imagine. For just as the heavens are higher than the earth, so my ways are higher than your ways and my thoughts higher than your thoughts" (Isa. 55:8–9, NLT).

The more I know him, my confidence increases to the point where there is an automatic recognition it is him I sense. His Spirit always brings peace, comfort, and leads to Truth, but God also convicts us of sin. There is a discomfort in the Spirit that God wants to help us be more like him. Though God's voice is gentle and kind, it is also powerful and life-changing.

I found a journal entry from 2007 where I was approached by someone wanting me to pray for her. She claimed to be desperate to hear God but didn't know when and what God was speaking to her.

I asked if she had prayed, and I appreciated her honesty when she said "no." *A desperation to hear God should instill a desire to talk to God.* People want to hear God, but they don't pray. It's quite simple; I talk to God and listen for the answer.

God's Voice to a Child

God has a heart to make himself known to everyone who longs to know him. I explained in my first book that when I was a child God drew me to himself with a longing to know him when I didn't fully know who God was. God did this with my nephew, Seth, who was nine at the time.

Seth sensed God's presence and did not question the Voice of God. What he heard, he believed, and believed without seeing. He seized the moment to know God more and held God's Word closely in his heart and mind.

"For me to doubt that God fills men with the Holy Spirit in answer to prayer would be thoroughly unscientific and irrational. I know he does. And in a matter like this, I would rather have one ounce of believing experience than ten tons of unbelieving exegesis" (Torrey, 1910).

There was no conscious effort on Seth's part when he heard God's voice for the first time. So often God's voice is in the silence, as was the case with Seth, but it was not so distance that he failed to recognize it was God. With unquestioning faith, Seth sat still and received God's voice supernaturally.

Seth's Story

Seth was preparing to enter the fourth grade and was eligible to attend church camp. After five days of camp, he came home exuberant from a personal encounter with God. He shared what God did for him during the week and unbeknownst to his mom, this wasn't the first time he heard the Voice of God. This was the second time Seth heard God's voice and from that first time, God prepared his little heart for what took place at camp.

Seth shared how God spoke to him, and he heard God. And he knew it was God. He experienced how God can rest upon our souls, which connects our spirit with God's spirit. Seth, whose heart was wide open for *all* of God, not just *some* of God, heard God again.

God's instructions were simple: "worship, praise, and prayer." He knew something special took place and God's goodness was too great to keep quiet. God is not a secret or something to be hidden.

"I am a different person. I am not myself. I feel different!" he said. How can a child comprehend what it means to be "different, changed"? God gave him those words to express his encounter with God. By the power and love of God who came from heaven to earth, personally, a nine-year-old can comprehend God's voice.

A few days later, he mentioned the deeper part of his connection to God. "You know, me and God have a thing. One day, he said my name while I was sitting at the computer, and I liked his voice. It was soft and quiet. He said, 'Focus only on me, praise me, and pray every day for your new house, and it will be your house.' The family had gone through a long process of buying their home. Ultimately, the house God prepared for them was beyond their wildest dreams. What a beautiful illustration for Seth to see answered prayers, from believing and expecting.

God's spirit prepared him, and Seth was a willing student in God's classroom, therefore, he had his first encounter of God's love and presence. We can never fully comprehend how beautiful God is, yet God is willing to give us an unexpected glimpse to know with certainty he is present. Seth believed what he *knew to be God's presence*. Seth's experience reveals the joy that comes in the relationship with Jesus Christ.

I want to have a *thing* going with God. I want to be so attuned to God coming to me before I go to him. If a nine-year-old can hear God in the middle of his fun-filled day, so can I. The faith of a child is most precious. He heard, he believed, he trusted (Matt. 18:3; Matt. 19:14).

Is it pride that causes us to remain silent to what God is doing? It never occurred to Seth that to share his God-story may come across as boastful. He didn't care if it sounded odd to others; he simply shared because he had his own experience to tell.

Humility—God's Way

"The person who wishes to boast should boast only of what the Lord has done" (1 Cor. 1:31, NLT).

God captures my attention in so many beautiful ways. He speaks through the words of a pastor, scripture, a whisper into my spirit, authors, but also through dreams and visions. I journal these beautiful encounters because I don't want to forget God's wonders and his direct involvement in my life. A look back into my spiritual journals allows me to see what God has done and ensures he receives the glory he deserves.

Jeremiah was instructed repeatedly by God to "write everything down word for word." In my book, *Beautiful Dreamer: Dreams—God's Personal Navigation System*, I shared the importance and value of keeping a spiritual journal. This is a means to strengthen our walk with God by looking back at answered prayers and words of encouragement.

God instructed Moses, Jeremiah, and others to record what he had done. These Old Testament men recorded God's intervention in their lives and countless people have benefited from it for over thousands of years. I want to keep my God-stories alive, so my children will do the same and so on to future generations. Therefore, I've included several journal entries from 1997, 1998, and other years for all to share in God's goodness. Out of this same discipline since my youth, God has enriched my walk with him as I can look back and see how clearly his hand has been over my life, protecting, loving, guiding.

As the years passed, God asked me a question over and over. "Why are you keeping me hidden? What I teach you is not meant to be a secret." He was so loving and patient with me, but he repeated this to me until I was ready to honestly deal with the answer. As I pondered this simple question, I could not ignore the truth. I had self-imposed limits on communicating to others what God was doing in my life.

Why? As a Christian I limited my public praise thinking it was humble by believing that boasting about what God has done in my life may appear pretentious to others. God opened my eyes and showed me this mentality results in dishonoring him through my silence.

God began teaching me that my apprehension to share the amazing things he does is nothing more than false humility. God's working power is not meant to be tucked away, safely hidden from others. There is "… A time to speak and a time to be silent" (Eccles. 3:7, NLT).

Remaining silent so as to appear humble is denying my Lord the glory he deserves. I "hide my candle under a bush." I believe "lighting a candle" not only includes the message of salvation, but also reveals the nature of God, in all his ways, in all places. I have the privilege to join all creation praising the King of kings.

"No one lights a lamp and then covers it with a washtub or shoves it under the bed … We're not keeping secrets; we're telling them. We're not hiding things; we're bringing everything out into the open. So be careful that you don't become misers of what you hear. Generosity begets generosity. Stinginess impoverishes" (Luke 8:16–28, MSG).

31

As I began writing this book, I continually struggled because it didn't come naturally for me to share my personal encounters with God so publicly. I realized the challenges I was experiencing were primarily due to my hesitation to openly and honestly declare the amazing things God has done!

Finally, I listened to hear with the goal to move to action and obedience. It was the same message when I began writing my first book. Patiently, God impressed upon my spirit, "Your journals, your journals." When I succumbed to God's clearly defined instructions to "write what I have shown you, what I've taught you" is when the overall purpose of this book began to pour out. Worship!

In 2000, I recorded in my journal the same hesitation about sharing the God-stories of my life and faith in Christ. No matter how many times God presented himself in such a personal manner; I was continually holding back from sharing the many ways he was operating in my life.

I recorded that if others were to pick up my journals and read my entries they may find my encounters with God odd, and they were. Yes odd, perhaps, by the standards of modern culture, but undeniable to me—"I know what God speaks to me. God is meant to be discovered and limiting my words of the Gospel is not humility," I wrote. I have stories to tell of God's mighty acts, and I want to be part of "everyone talking" about God's marvelous wonders. God wants me to communicate the variety in which he displays his love and communicates his direction.

Several months after God began piercing my heart to reveal more of what he has shown me beyond my first book, I came across the book, *Breaking the Veil of Silence,* by Jobst Bittner, a beautiful account how God is continuing to heal families and communities from the effects of World War II and the Holocaust.

The perpetrators, as well as the victims, asked for forgiveness, with detailed accounts of the pain they endured. The power of silence is broken and healing can take place across Europe after generations of the bondage of silence.

"It is about time we break free from old family (including church) patterns. We no longer have to live with them. It is only when we put our experiences into words as precisely as possible, giving them their proper name, that we will finally be able to break this veil" (Bittner, 2013, p. 88). This is especially true for God's children.

Should I lift my own veil of silence about the wonder of God? If so, how, when? God's Word tells us that signs and wonders will follow the word of our testimony (Mark 16:20). It is through our testimony, boasting in the One and Only Living God, that people will be saved. In Revelations, it states it is through our "bold testimony."

It is my belief God wants each of us to boast of his magnificence. "You made me so happy, God I saw your work and I shouted for joy. How magnificent your work, God" (Ps. 92:4, MSG). God stirred within my heart a need to shout for joy for, over, and about who he is and all he has done for me. He gently whispered, "Why don't you allow me to choose the how, when, and with whom, not the other way around? Let me write your story." Again, a question from God I needed to ponder and an action I needed to take.

I wish I could say my lips have boasted in God more often in my lifetime than they were involved in negativity, gossip, and pessimism. Many times I have sought God's forgiveness for speaking without thinking. Yet, when it comes to God's goodness and greatness, I too easily hide behind this veil of false humility, limiting my public praise of his glory.

I find it easy to talk about my children. I try to humbly share their accomplishments when they make good choices. Most parents and grandparents don't hesitate to boast in their children and grandchildren. My dear friends know I welcome listening to them because I know their children personally. I want the best for them the way I know they want the same for me. There is great joy in sharing the good without the intention to point fingers at the failures of others.

It's this same joy talking about God that I don't want to hesitate in sharing. My friends encourage me through their testimonies of how God is working in their lives. Sincere bragging isn't self-centered but reveals the love you have for another. This is how I'm trying to approach revealing the incredible mysteries and wonders of my God.

If I'm not talking about what God produces within my soul and mind, which include dreams, visions, a whisper, how will others know he does? How does my silence teach people how they can experience God intimately and personally? They won't! Hiding behind this veil shrouds my lips to speak forth all the amazing things the Lord does.

I want to be like David when he said, "With every bone in my body I will praise him" (Ps. 35:10, NLT).

The Bible states the whole earth worships and praises the Lord. I want a readiness in my heart and lips to brag on God without reservation. I don't want to hesitate to boast in God's magnificence and to do so publicly. Too often, silence wins. This book is an effort to change that.

There are numerous accounts in the Bible where God revealed his presence and character in a variety of ways. These accounts in the Bible and the stories recorded there are what encourage me to rely on God.

The more I earnestly seek God for who he is, the more I experience an increase of seeing and hearing him. Out of this, God has sealed his Word of approval to remove my veil of silence and embolden me to boast about the variety of his nature.

THE MORE I EARNESTLY SEEK GOD FOR WHO HE IS,
THERE IS AN INCREASE OF SEEING AND HEARING HIM.

God grew a desire in my heart to boast of him outwardly, not just privately, and it has been from this that God continues to prompt my heart to boast of his nature without inhibition. God ignited my spirit to move forward publicly through *Love of the Cross Vision*.

I've glimpsed God's grace and goodness through the years, which has come from an outgrowth of his sweet presence. Jesus is

Truth, reveals Truth, and wants me to share his Truth. To know God personally is to know his glory.

If I don't know God personally, I won't experience or see his glory. If I don't see his glory, I can't share in his glory. If I don't share in his glory, I ask myself, "Do I know him"?

I've discovered no other way of knowing God and seeing his nature than to put myself in a place where I can experience his presence. It is from time with God that I can then share the good news of Christ, for his glory.

God in all his glory is magnificent, beautiful, leaving me speechless so many times. His presence is unmistakable and nothing short of fantastic! He is the wonder of the cross, the wonder in the Name, and the wonder of my heart. God is personal, inviting, and desires to be the wonder of my heart so I can reveal the incredible, loving God of heaven and earth.

I turned my attention to my journals with a new perspective.

"If any of you are embarrassed over me and the way I'm leading you when you get around your fickle and unfocused friends, know that you'll be an even greater embarrassment to the Son of Man when he arrives in all the splendor of God, his Father, with an army of the holy angels" (Mark 8:38, MSG).

I knew exactly what God was speaking and asking me to do. I continued to ponder God's questions with the intent to change my behavior, yet I continued to repeat this same tendency to keep my lips sealed and share less, not more.

I kept asking God as though he had never answered. My frustration grew because I was not listening to *obey* God's simple instructions.

I didn't start this book with the goal of having the majority of my stories be about signs and wonders. Nevertheless, the more I wrote in obedience to God and to honor him, the more my intimate moments with God revealed his invisible qualities. His creativity. How God was reaching into the center of my soul and the new work he was doing in and through me was unmistakable. God asked me to share and by stepping into obedience he gave me *more* God-stories to report.

The words contained within the pages of my spiritual journal were the following: "Reveal who I am. Express how my presence is real and necessary," he spoke. "Give to the Lord the glory he deserves" (Ps. 96:8, NLT). When I see Jesus face-to-face I want to be found worthy of one who obeyed his Spirit's direction fully, especially how he desires to reach deep into the soul and pierce our hearts with a new revelation of who he is. It was time to be more transparent.

Paul beautifully described in Romans how God uses his children to bring the Good News to others through our boasting. "For I am, by God's grace, a special messenger ... So it is right for me to be enthusiastic about all Christ Jesus has done through me in my service to God. I dare not boast of anything else. I [Paul] have won them over by the miracles done through me as signs from God—all by the power of God's Spirit. In this way, I have fully presented the Good News of Christ" (Rom. 15:15–19, NLT).

My journals revealed how I had in times past praised and acknowledged God's sovereignty—his goodness, forgiveness, kindness, etc. However, sadness overtook me as I realized the work God had been doing in my life remained hidden from others.

It became evident to me that the majority of my life I had obeyed only part of what God was calling me to do. I was sharing in his glory, but I wasn't sharing the full extent of his glory. God was gently guiding me to share the Good News of Christ with abandon.

IF I DON'T KNOW HIS GLORY, I DON'T SEE HIS GLORY.
IF I DON'T SEE HIS GLORY, I CAN'T SHARE HIS GLORY.

A delicate balance began about what and how to boast in God. How do I pay tribute for all he has done? I did not want to be disobedient and guilty or leave a "stone unturned" but to share God with others and with excitement. My joy and confidence stemmed only from prayer and God repeated to me that my time and obligation were to him alone and no other.

If I were to hold back was I ashamed? In Matthew 6, Jesus teaches us how to pray. Before Jesus gave us the simple Lord's Prayer, he gave instructions that we are to pray in secret and not to be seen by man. This was to prevent the sin of pride and false appearance of piety. It was the motive of the heart he was addressing. I also think this passage teaches us that the growth of our relationship comes in private intimacy with God.

God's Word also tells us there are things he reveals that we are to express. Matthew 10:23–27 states, "The things I tell you in the dark you must say in the daylight, and the things you hear in your private ear you must proclaim from the house-tops" (Phillps).

What I was to share seemed to go against the *grain* of Jesus's message to remain in private. Surely not everything in the secret place of prayer is meant for public disclosure. However, I can rest knowing what God speaks to me in the private place of prayer includes direction as to when to reveal and take action and when to unveil the beauty of God.

Again, God was reminding me not to concern myself with what man may think. Paul wrote in 1 Corinthians 4:3 of his faithfulness to share the Good News and "it matters very little what you or anyone else thinks. I don't even trust my own judgment on this point. My conscience is clear, but that isn't what matters. It is the Lord himself who will examine me and decide" (NLT).

Others may find foolishness in the transparency to reveal the secrets of his heart. However, to those who "have the mind of Christ," will receive, with excitement, how God works in our lives when we are open to receive (1 Cor. 3:16, NLT).

With God's help, I made the decision to publicly communicate the abundance of his presence, regardless if others may find the moving of the Spirit strange and foreign. It was time to share more of the secrets of his heart and how my delight in him can be the delight of all.

It is *only* through time in God's presence that I can have confidence to proclaim God's Word and join creation in applauding all God is and does. I cannot bypass the importance of active prayer. Through prayer, God opened many doors and turned mere words into miracles.

R. A. Torrey expresses the Person in his book, *The Person and Work of The Holy Spirit,* "Before one can correctly understand the work of the Holy Spirit, he must first of all know the Spirit himself … decide whether the Holy Spirit is a Divine Person, worthy to receive our adoration, our faith, our love, and our entire surrender to himself … If the Holy Spirit is a Person, and a Divine Person, and we do not know him as such, then we are robbing a Divine Being of the worship and the faith and the love and the surrender to himself which are his due" (1910).

I want to give away what God has given freely to me and take his message beyond my four walls and into the streets. To do so, I must know the person, Jesus Christ. My motive for writing is simply this: I want you to enjoy this, too, so that your joy will double my joy!" (1 John 1:1–4, MSG).

Looking back at the amazing blessings during times with God excites me! There is no greater joy than to be in unity with him and have the privilege to be a member of the body of Christ. I have no doubt God wants to equip me so I can attain an unshakeable faith in God my Father.

Having an unshakeable faith in God does not come from silence, especially not from a false sense of humility. I want to honor God every day, and he has taught me that I can do so by sharing the stories of his grace, mighty acts, and wonders. In essence, God was telling me to be forward thinking by first looking back and *never forgetting the former things from God.*

Now I plunged into my journals with an eagerness to share my stories. I could no longer restrain my excitement to tell about the amazing things God has and is doing (Ps. 96:4, NLT). What I had kept close to my heart for most of my life, hidden within the pages of my spiritual journals, I knew God wanted me to proclaim this evidence of his goodness, love, and gentleness. I worked to give God the glory he deserves.

"As a Christian, I am not governed by diplomacy or policy or public opinion. I am governed by what the Lord has said in my heart by revelation as to his purpose ... It is a ministry by revelation" (Sparks, 1973).

Part 2

Celestial Vision to Worship

3

Power of God vs. the Power of Technology

One of the primary barriers to growing in our relationship with God and continually experiencing his hidden nature is a lack of spending time with him. The more time we spend fellowshipping with the Triune God, the more we hunger and thirst for him. The less time we spend, the more comfortable we are to ignore God. Often it takes a crisis for us to reach into our little-god closet hoping that God Almighty will come to our rescue.

We seek growth, efficiency, and the new in so many other areas of our life. When a new technology is available, we reach for it immediately. When a new social media site becomes popular, we rush to set up an account. We tell our friends; we want them to buy into the "new" so that they can share our experience.

For me, it's necessary to evaluate how much time I spend with God as opposed to manmade tools and technology. The Bible should be *the Go-to*. Often, we rely on God the way we rely on applications (apps) on our phone. We go to him when we need him and we ignore him when we have no perceived need for him.

My mobile device has an audible notification when I receive a call, text, or e-mail, which gets my attention. Too often I miss the "ding" of God drawing me to him and getting my attention. I had to ask myself, "Do I wake up and look to God or my phone first?" I was trying to do the former, but I had to admit I didn't always look to God first when it comes to how I function on a daily basis.

I had to be honest about how the thrill of technology often overrides a newness with God. I don't look for the many ways God wants to operate in my life that would actually make my day and situations less stressful and more efficient.

Too often I function and settle with what I have known of God, and I don't intentionally look for more within God's endless possibilities. It seems I'm not willing to accept all he offers.

I have had moments in my life where my time with God seemed repetitive, even boring. God wants me to see him anew and to interact with him on a regular basis.

"Do I get stuck in a rut, not recognizing how God wants to make himself available to me? Don't I want God's best so he can operate through me?" I asked myself. There was no question that I do; however, how I spend my time might indicate otherwise. Accepting or buying the tools of technology doesn't mean I use it any more than saying I'm a believer and accept all who God is. I knew God wanted me to see more of him and tap into what he wants to do for and through me.

For my benefit, God has given me free and complete access for a creative, interactive, and entertaining dialogue and experience with him. God is all-knowing and full of information and knowledge essential to living a God-empowered life.

There are many times the technology that I rely on daily freezes and malfunctions. The best part of relying fully on God is that I will never experience "no service." He is always present, available, and willing.

I must pay with my time, which begins with prayer and reading the Bible if I want to see how God wants to work creatively through me. There must be a desire to give God my all on a daily basis.

I don't want my relationship with Christ to look like yesterday. And, I don't want today's walk with God to be the same as tomorrow. I want worship to become my lifestyle. I want to be swept into the presence of God.

*"Prayer is real work. Prayer is vital work ... There may be
the exhibit, the circumstance, and the pomp of praying, and
yet no real praying. There may be much attitude, gesture,
and verbiage, but no praying" (Bounds, 2000, p. 230).*

It was from this perspective, God began to instill in me more of
his presence in ways I had not previously experienced. "This is the
kind of God I have and I'm telling the world" (Exod. 15:1–8, MSG).

God wanted me to search for him and see him with a fresh and
fun outlook each day. Yes, I said, "fun!" If God created everything,
he designed fun too! Technology entertains me, but so does God.
I've been experiencing a whole new level of fun when I spend time
in prayer and reading the Bible. My worship has become interactive
and nothing short of fantastic!

The Bible says that heaven is a place of rejoicing and joy. I have
had many occasions where joy and fun with friends has caused me to
belly laugh until I ache. Our guide to pray "on earth as it is in heaven"
includes praying the joy of heaven to earth and into my life (Matt.
6:10). Fun is just one of the many wonderful things God has awakened
me to in the heavenly realm that cannot be explained in the natural.

Through prayer and worship, God revealed more of the extraordinary God he is and the infinite blessings of being in his presence
that I still find hard to describe!

God began pushing me to boast in him without hesitation,
including those unusual encounters. The more I recognize God in all
areas of my life, the more there is an inexplicable joy and excitement
I have to help people recognize the variety of God's mighty acts of
endless possibilities.

*I can only boast of what I know, use regularly, and am familiar
with. I want to be a God-boaster and express and proclaim
his character, love, grace, tenderness, and mighty works.*

God taught me it is necessary to intentionally remove the distractions in life that get in the way of enjoying him. I think one of the

biggest distractions is technology, but also other routines that don't fit God into my schedule. I had to be willing to recognize what I value most in my day. I needed to remove barriers and many of those barriers were the need to disconnect from technology and connect with God. I needed to quiet my soul and my surroundings.

It's not that we set aside everything in our day to be with him, but that we seek him, to honor him, to bring him glory, to speak with him throughout our day as we go about our daily tasks.

God must be key to all our thoughts and actions; thereby, we have a guarantee we will succeed in what we need to accomplish each and every day. Proverbs 16:3 states, "Commit your actions to the Lord, and your plans will succeed" (NLT).

As I became more intentional in my worship with God, unexpectedly, he began to enlarge my vision of worship. My style of worship began to change. From this, God revealed another beautiful image.

A Vision toward Organic Worship

"God takes particular pleasure in acts of worship—a different kind of "sacrifice"—that take place in kitchen and workplace and on the streets (Heb. 13:16, MSG).

Sometimes people ask, "What's God doing new in your life today?" In the past, I felt like I needed to conjure up something, because the reality was, I hadn't spent time with God, which meant I hadn't heard a fresh word from him.

I have seen a pattern in my walk with God when I live a life of spiritual mediocrity. The saving knowledge of Jesus Christ and the honor he deserves gets pushed aside because I've limited my times of prayer and absorbing the Word of God. Gradually, my spirit accepts no accountability or responsibility to share God and his ways. The worst of it is, I don't have anything new and exciting to share about what my God is doing. This responsibility is on me, not God.

No matter how old I get, when I do not seek God regularly, I wander through life with an attitude of indifference. A passive relationship with God results in a lack of desire for more of God. "We ought, therefore, to pay the greatest attention to the truth that we have heard and not allow ourselves to drift away from it" (Heb. 2:1, Phillips).

Further, when there is no depth in my relationship with Christ, I lack spiritual strength, and it's easy to regress to become an uncultivated and unproductive believer. Mediocrity breeds complacency, and I become satisfied with a form of faith that has no power. Worse, I may dismiss how much I need him and lack clarity for what his will is for my life.

It's simple. Yet periods of time can pass, even now, when it is easy to be lulled into complacency and mediocrity walking with the Spirit. Without God's presence, a sermon, or even the Word of God has limited impact to change and help me. It is only through personal time with God and making him my constant companion that I can take the path of spiritual progress. Spiritual progress doesn't come from believing in God or going to church. It's a life of faith in action. It is obedience.

I want spiritual progress. To live a God-centered life for the purpose of sharing the salvation provided only by Christ. There is no progress in my spirit without intentionally giving God permission to trim that which must be removed and hinders growth. By remaining connected to Christ, I can thrive in and for the Kingdom for the glory of God.

God wanted to broaden my spiritual senses through a new path of simple worship—a fresh way of honoring his being. God supernaturally deposited in my heart, mind, body, and soul a desire to worship him in a new way and from it, he created a deeper longing for his nearness.

I have asked God many times, if man was created to honor him through worship why doesn't it come instinctively? There have been numerous occasions I've prayed and invited the Holy Spirit into the room, whether alone or in corporate worship. Why would I need to invite God where he already resides? God showed me that even though I acknowledge that he is always present, there is still a need within my natural being that I have to work my way into worship. If it doesn't come naturally, how can I worship without "working" my way there? Why do I have to work my way into worship if I am God's most precious creation, *intended* to worship him?

"What does worshipping God, look like for me?" I kept asking. "How can I worship you instinctively?" The Bible states that all God's creation, from heaven to earth, worships the Lord God Almighty. Yet too often I hesitate because it feels manufactured.

The more I asked God about this part of human nature, it was evident he had already begun guiding me, beginning with the *Love of the Cross Vision*. He was answering my prayers though I wasn't recognizing this yet. I believe this stirring in my spirit was God's way of directing my attention to lavish him with my love the way he lavishes his love over me.

Discerning more and more of God's presence came with the prerequisite to love him and his Word more than ever. God's specific guidance began with worship, praise, and prayer in an entirely new way. I began to come to him with worship as a verb.

Worshipping in spirit and truth begins with my attitude. It's giving God my best, whether praising him during church, taking communion, striving to obey his commandments, or giving of my tithe and offering. Now God was stirring something in my spirit to see worship as something more, something living, something active.

God was slowly teaching me to rid myself of manmade rules, while remaining within the confines of his perfect Word, the Bible. "Look to and for me, not man," God impressed upon my spirit. "Our religion is little because our god is little. Our religion is weak because our god is weak … We do not see God as he is" (Tozer, 1997, p. 41). I want to see God as he is, in all things, in all ways, if he so chooses to reveal himself.

What stemmed from prayer became a pictorial, instructional process on how to worship God. The image of the cross became my process flowchart, bringing a fresh look at God's existence, nature, character, and love for me personally.

I understood the cross and worship in the years that ensued after I accepted Christ. This, however, was a fresh, God-guided journey toward knowing him in ways that awakened my senses to feel, see, and hear him. *Really hear him.*

There is no blueprint to worship, but God began revealing a need to look closer at what redemption looks like for the sole purpose of worship. He was "fanning the flames" of my heart to worship with intensity I had not put forth in times past. God put a fire in my spirit, a burning zeal and a new perspective that worship doesn't have to be stale, repetitive, or uneventful.

When it came to my private time with God, I had to learn how to cultivate an atmosphere where worship flowed naturally so God could manifest himself in all his fullness. By doing so, his Spirit was and is always recognizable. The Word is alive, but abiding in the presence of God is power. And this power results in faith, which results in action!

While reading the writings of Brother Lawrence, a seventeenth century monk, God reinforced the message sealed in my heart: "Why should we be satisfied with a brief moment of worship? With such meager devotion, we restrain the flow of God's abundant grace. If God can find a soul filled with a lively faith, he pours his grace into it in a torrent which, having found an open channel, gushes out exuberantly" (Lawrence, 2008).

The Word is living, but living in the presence of God is power, and this power results in faith, which results in action.

As I move forward with God, he faithfully develops an appetite deep within my soul that cannot be satisfied elsewhere. God revealing himself, helping me remove my "veil of silence" in order to brag of his loving nature. The more I brag on God, the more my hunger for God increases. It is the Holy Spirit's fire that strengthens me for a God-progress life.

When I look to him with expectation, he teaches and also surprises me, time and time again. Throughout my life, I've quoted the verse from Psalm 34:8: "O taste and see that the Lord is good" (KJV).

In *The Message* it states, "Open your mouth and taste, open your eyes and see—how good God is. Blessed are you who run to him." I serve an extraordinary God who desires to awaken me to things in the heavenly realm.

I don't believe it is only a metaphor. I keep my heart open to see God manifest himself, so I can "taste and see" his glory. God is creator of all and he will choose and validate his Word in many different ways.

I had one experience, one of those peculiar moments with God, when I was sitting on my bed, Bible open on my lap, when God spoke a gentle word of instruction. I say peculiar because it was a metaphor how God wanted me to view the Bible.

God said to "caress and devour the Word, eat it like a scroll." It isn't enough to hear a verse from a sermon or a song; I must have an "appetite" that craves the knowledge of God. I must have a fondness, a tenderness to the Word and keep it close to my heart. *When I know the Word, I know God. When I read the Word, I hear God.*

It was a special moment where God used two symbols (caress and devour) to awaken my senses and to convey a powerful message. I must consume every part of God, especially God's commands and instructions.

When God enlarged my vision toward celebrating him anew, he awakened my entire being in the natural realm with his supernatural presence of sight, sound, and touch one morning. The power of God changed the atmosphere in my home with his tangible presence.

The only way I can describe how my senses are touched by the heart of God would be to compare it to how I feel during times of great joy or sorrow. Often my physical body feels light as a feather that moves me to laugh uncontrollably. Or sometimes I feel as though a weight is resting on my heart, the pain of a situation so intense.

The touch of God is a mysterious phenomenon and it is difficult to express unless you have your own encounter with God. When someone believes on the name of Jesus to save him and deliver him from sin, so often there is an immediate sense of freedom physically and emotionally. His spirit springs to life. It is not seen with physical eyes, but it is felt deep within the soul.

What I have to share with others about who my God is comes most often during my times of simple conversation with God. The few visions I have had are straightforward, no hidden riddles, but colorful images where God makes himself known. Words are heard, but there are also times of silence. Either way, I've found visions rarely need clarification because the message of the vision has come with such clarity.

I serve an extraordinary God who awakens
me to things in the heavenly realm.

During a time I was giving honor to God, he sharpened my spiritual eyes to see and experience in the natural, a glimpse of heaven. God captured my heart and revealed himself in a beautiful and unexpected way. Not only as Father, God to child, but friend-to-friend. It felt as though I had crossed the threshold of heaven.

The more I worshipped and embraced God, connecting my heart to his, a passion grew, and he raptured my heart with one of my most cherished visions. It is one of enchantment and delight, which was and is the ultimate beauty from the *Love of the Cross* Vision.

It was as though the heavens opened and I had my own intimate moment, basking in God's presence and splendor. God took my breath away as he so often does—something so glorious, never to be forgotten. I call it my *Celestial Vision*.

For God, who said, "Let there be light in the darkness," has made
us understand that this light is the brightness of the glory of God
that is seen in the face of Jesus Christ (2 Cor. 4:6, NLT).

Celestial Vision

In this vision, the heavens opened and by the Spirit of the Lord, God made himself known. I saw his white clothing, no face, but his crown and ray of light, his glory in every direction. The white was unlike what I've seen in the natural realm. A brilliance, but not blinding. A cloud of unadulterated purity. I was walking side-by-side, hand-in-hand, with Jesus. I could only see his white robe, no face. No words were shared, just moving forward, never backward. I seemed to recognize this as an important element of our walk. As I soaked in his celestial presence and beauty, I praised him for who he is, for what he is, for his gentleness, patience, love, kindness, forgiveness, mercy. My mind could think of nothing else, but to worship him. As we walked in silence, I could feel his warmth and within my spirit I understood all of who he is instantaneously. It is indescribable because everything I felt and perceived about who God is was as quick as the blink of an eye. His divine presence revealed with silence. Immense love and peace permeated my surroundings. He never spoke a word, but words weren't necessary. God does not need to defend who he is.

End of vision

Once again, God took my breath away. Taking one's *breath* away means to "be overwhelmed by someone or something where beauty or grandeur surprises or astounds someone" (Dictionary.com, 2015).

It was during a time spent in prayer and praising God for who he is, that he willingly and graciously gave me this glimpse of his beauty. God didn't have to legitimize who he was in that moment, but he did affirm who he is. He gave me a peek into the richness of his love, and his peace pervaded my heart and mind.

The way God communicated to me in that moment was different than in times past when God put one word, one sentence, or an instruction understandable in the human mind. In this vision, there was no sentence or isolated word, but the nature of his being was captured in one momentary thought.

I asked God again if he created man to worship him, to help me do so naturally and effortlessly. He began teaching me the importance of regularly and literally bowing my head or kneeling before him in the privacy of my home. Bowing creates humility and it was how God began expanding my view of how to worship and honor him.

I've bowed many times in prayer, but most often it's in church. I don't have to bow, but God was teaching me not to deviate from his instructions. There should be no exceptions to obeying God's requests.

Looking for God to manifest himself supernaturally did not mean I was looking for an encounter of enlightenment to take me to a "state" away from God. I wasn't on a self-seeking, "I've seen the light," moment, though others may want to define it as such. The Bible says that "Satan masquerades as an angel of light" (2 Cor. 11:14, KJV). Satan has to masquerade because there is no light or hope found in him. However, Jesus is not only *a* light, but *the* Light. I was focusing on the light of Jesus.

When there is confusion, it isn't God because Satan tries to divert the supernatural onto himself. Peace and light are not Satan's characteristics. When peace is present, there's no doubt it is God and from God.

My *Celestial Vision* came from learning to worship God anew and being open to different ideas of what worship can look like. It was another way God wanted to transform my worship, even though I didn't know it needed transformation.

It was through worship God opened the heavens and brought the atmosphere of heaven to me personally. I first had to learn to honor God personally and privately. How long will we wait for a glimpse of an earthly celebrity or famous politician? Will we wait that long for a true glimpse of the Maker of heaven and earth, who is the King of kings?

Only the Scriptures can accurately describe my thoughts and emotions from my open heaven experience. Open heaven is what Peter experienced in Acts 10:11. Peter "… fell into a trance. He saw the sky open, and something like a large sheet was let down by its four corners" (NLT).

There are several scripture verses that show how God will open our eyes to see the spiritual things of heaven and the revelations that happen when sitting in his presence.

David Orton explains "open heaven" as "… an unhindered manifestation in the earth of all that heaven is, of God's own presence and glory. Natural laws can be temporarily or permanently suspended as heaven breaks in. Signs and wonders, miracles and healings, revelations and unusual manifestations of power begin to occur …" (Orton, August 27, 2014).

In that moment, the display of God's brilliance was and is beyond comparison.

My words cannot adequately describe the beauty how God dazzled me with the splendor of his glorious presence that morning. He is Light, his brilliance as bright as the sun fills the whole earth, and he fills me. I love when I worship God how he instills within me a desire to expect revelation, a visitation, him to inhabit my entire being.

Another beautiful description from the Bible describing God in the heavens is found in Psalm 104:1–3: "O Lord my God, You are very great: You are clothed with honor and majesty, who cover Yourself with light as with a garment, who stretch out the heavens like a curtain. He lays the beams of his upper chambers in the waters, who makes the clouds his chariot, who walks on the wings of the wind …" (NKJV).

In the days that followed the *Celestial Vision,* God confronted me with the need for outrageous praise. He began to challenge me to come before him without inhibition as the way to begin boasting in him. I was learning to be captivated by his loving presence from the illustration of his friendship.

When I removed the barriers about how worship should look, it was then that I was able to worship God organically. *Organic* means "denoting a relation between elements of something such that they fit together harmoniously as necessary parts of a whole" (Dictionary. com, 2015).

Time with God began looking drastically and consistently different. Through an increased desire to honor God, he guided my heart to unrestrained worship, and an ever-increasing appreciation for the cross.

It was me and God that morning. "I began to live as if there were no one but God and myself in the world" (Lawrence, 2008). Nothing else mattered. No person mattered more than God himself.

I was to continue taking time to boast in who God is and what he has done and does. "I praise you for …" and I couldn't stop listing everything he means to me. With each passing day, I saw a fresh outlook to the glory of God coming down from heaven and into my world. "His will be done on earth as it is in heaven," I praised.

God inhabited my mind and spirit and my heart continued to say, "Praise the name of the Lord!"

I love asking God to "invigorate my soul," and it's exactly what God began doing. I want to hold onto God until he fills all my senses. I want to walk away and know I've touched the heart of God and his love has touched me.

This beautiful *Celestial Vision*, which stemmed from worship, is what invigorated my soul and roused my spirit for more of God.

> *Let praise cascade off my lips … I love it when you show yourself! Invigorate my soul so I can praise you well, use your decrees to put iron in my soul!" (Ps. 119:169–176, MSG).*

God's Endless Creativity

I remember feeling this same awe of God's beauty when I saw the Sistine Chapel in Rome. It is estimated that over five million tourists (five million souls) pass through the Sistine Chapel annually. I listened to the audio recording, viewing Michelangelo's paintings on the wall outlining the events in the Bible from Genesis to Revelation. I stood in awe of how it proclaims creation and acknowledges Jesus, Son of God, crucified, resurrected, and that the only way to heaven is through Christ.

Right there, I had to sit down. The message so powerful! This is, no doubt, an anointed work of God. To have a visual painting, summarizing Genesis to Revelation, pierced my heart with fresh understanding of God's love for all mankind and his plan to redeem us. The room was filled, shoulder-to-shoulder, with visitors from all over the world. In that moment God was speaking into my spirit how the souls standing in the crowded room were hearing the message of Salvation through Jesus Christ, perhaps for the first time.

Taking in what was before me, my heart also ached seeing all those faces, recognizing many were hearing the name of Jesus for the first time. All those listening to the audio tour were receiving the message of the Gospel that the only way to heaven is through Jesus Christ. In a small way this experience helps me understand how God feels joy and pain simultaneously, the way Jesus did on the cross.

I prayed for those in the room where I stood, hoping one day I would know them personally in heaven because they recognized God was The One True God through this beautiful masterpiece. "He stretches out the skies like a canvas" (Isa. 40:22, MSG). God desires none should perish (1 Pet. 3:5).

Everywhere I go, he is.

There will never be a duplicate of Michelangelo's remarkable frescoes, and this original artist reminded me of how God is also an artist and he is very creative. *His creativity is what makes him personal.* Though experiences and encounters with God may be similar, God speaks to me as an individual and in a language that resonates with my life. He does this for each of us.

God had given me another glimpse of how every tongue will worship him automatically while standing in his presence. There will be only one response and that is to acknowledge his supreme being. Recognizing how God takes me into his presence to do nothing but acknowledge his Supreme Being is thrilling, but it will be unimaginably greater when I see the whole world bowing as all creation acknowledges his Kingship together as The One True God.

I want to worship him with all my might now and proclaim the great news. I will continue to boast in him with a loud voice, shouting to the world, Jesus is King of kings, Lord of lord's, Ruler of all, Redeemer, Deliverer, Counselor, my Banner, Righteousness, Strength, Tower, Lover of my soul.

I want to be an empty canvas and let God choose how he will create something new in me for his glory—for others to look on and see that he is good. By allowing God to reveal himself his way, he lovingly displays his creativity, including through supernatural images of his beauty.

The world needs hope and hope is found in the cross, in Jesus. The *Love of the Cross Vision* became the foundation by which worship became effortless, followed by walking hand-in-hand, beholding his celestial beauty.

God's goodness is so great I had no idea the beauty of his presence would continue to come to me regularly as he guided me to worship.

> *"O Lord, what a variety of things you have made!…Every one of these depends on you to give …" (Ps. 104:24, NLT).*

Runaway Worship

> *"We want to see, want to have, we want the proofs and the evidences. We do really, after all, want a kingdom that can be appraised by our senses of sight and hearing and feeling—a palpable kingdom, the answer in tangible form to all our efforts and labors; and the opposite of that is a tremendous strain upon faith, and sometimes even brings us to serious crisis" (Sparks, 2000, p. 116,).*

Every day of every year is a new and exciting journey with God as I am willing to embrace the heart of God. Learning to be in conversation with the Father, enjoying time with him, waiting and walking in his presence becomes more natural the more I practice it.

The enemy of my soul wants to keep my praise withdrawn, standing alone in isolated prayer, but God desires that I am willing to step into effortless worship. The more I worship, the more I recognize how the enemy wants to silence my praise and thanks to God.

In the days, weeks, and months that followed my image of the *Love of the Cross Vision*, I continued to examine and scrutinize every detail of the cross. It was the birth of a new and exciting spiritual journey. A teaching to embrace and be attached to his heavenliness with "all I've got" (Israel & New Breed's, 2012)! There was a continual recognition of the limitations I had unknowingly placed on how to worship God in the privacy of my home. Was I resistant to change when it came to worship? I didn't think so.

"The Church represents Jesus, which basically means to re-present him. If we can host him, and in the process become like him, then perhaps the world will actually experience 'it's My kindness that leads you to repentance'." (Johnson, 2012, p. 63).

As the days and months passed, God nourished my soul through scripture, dreams, and visions. My dreams are so vivid and full of color I don't think the way my dreams play out! I'm amazed at how God plants such imaginative dreams in my mind! My brain does not operate in an artistic way. Yet, the dreams I have and the stories within them leave me with no doubt they are God-dreams.

Through a habit of devoted time with God, he began teaching me how to increase "practicing the presence of God" (Lawrence, 2008). God planted intensity in my spirit to come before him in a variety of ways. He began calling me to a deeper, more intimate relationship by literally placing my entire being in a disposition to be close to his heart.

As I changed my posture to stand when God said stand, God humbled me, exalted himself, and brought me into his presence in unpredictable ways. Most people never experience God directing their physical worship, but it's an open invitation to all.

It started from the passage in John 4:23-34: "It's who you are and the way you live that count before God. Your worship must engage your spirit in the pursuit of truth. That's the kind of people the Father is out looking for: those who are simply and honestly themselves before him in their worship. God is sheer being itself—Spirit. Those who worship him must do it out of their very being, their spirits, their true selves, in adoration" (MSG).

Engage leaped off the pages. God was prodding me to worship him with more zeal and pursue him with my very being. Then I read Romans 12. Three words lifted off the pages, "give your body," complemented what God was speaking into my spirit from John 4. There was a consistent message for me directed at worship. God was rearranging and reinforcing my mental model of how he is able and willing to escort me into his presence.

Worship has to be active. I find when a pastor asks the congregation to stand, most stand. When he or she asks the crowd to raise one or two hands, the majority do even though it often feels awkward. God was telling me to behave the same when he gives me the instructions in the privacy of my home. God was pushing me toward true worship expressed from my entire being, not only from words or in the quietness of my heart.

In times past, I had come to God with my whole being by bowing or raising my hands, but I must be honest and state that most often it was short-lived. My normal routine with God was sitting quietly, Bible open, praying. It wasn't wrong, but God wanted to stretch me.

God wanted me to put into action those verses stating I am to love him with all my strength and being. To love God with my entire soul and mind. It is equally important to love and worship him with my physical body, which may include changing my posture during times of prayer. God was broadening my spiritual senses from my inner being to his Being.

I recognized I needed to surrender my physical worship and be willing to present my entire being (demeanor) before the Lord. By doing so, a spontaneous stirring in my spirit occurred. Andrew Murray calls a full surrender resulting in "spontaneous expression," and this is where I met God spirit-to-spirit (Murray, 1898).

God was teaching me how to love him with all my might. Desiringgod.org provides a beautiful picture what this can mean to each of us. The word, *might* or *strength* translates in Deuteronomy 6:5 usually functions as the adverb *very* in the Old Testament. It not only shows up in the Old Testament it is referenced 298 times. The noun version occurs in Deuteronomy and in only one other place, which itself is just an echo of our passage.

In 2 Kings 23:25, we are told that King Josiah "turned to Yahweh with all his heart and with all his soul and with all his might." So if the word usually means "very." What would it mean to love the Lord will all our "very-ness"? Interestingly, the Greek translation of this word is "power." The Aramaic translation is "wealth." Both of these may actually be pointing in the same direction, for the strength of a person is not simply who he is but what he has at his disposal (desiringgod.org).

This spontaneous reaction became runaway worship, resulting in a continual flow of refreshing and nourishment to my soul. In my pursuit to acknowledge God with a fresh outlook, he pursued me and over the next year my family and I experienced many promises, resulting in multiple miracles.

Empty Me of Me—Occupy My Soul, Lord

"God has taken you through it, and you know it like that. It is not that you have achieved something, but rather that you have been broken in the process. Now you are fit for something in the Lord" (Sparks, 2012).

When a president or a guest of honor enters a room the crowd usually gives a standing ovation. All eyes are on him or her. This is the attitude in which God was teaching me to come before him. Standing puts my eyes and heart on God and symbolically standing "before him" gives him the honor he deserves. Beginning with worship, prayer, and reading the Bible, standing was becoming a key path to acknowledging God's beauty.

One morning as I was worshipping God, his presence hovered over me in a powerful way. I took the same posture that I had in previous mornings, sitting at my kitchen table with my Bible open.

I was taking time to meditate on the Word, praying and keeping my mind from wandering on anything else but God. Sitting in silence, I felt he wanted me to stand in my kitchen. Once again God brought to mind the importance of engaging my *body* and spirit in pursuit of him. God wanted me to literally interact with him. Nobody was looking thank goodness!

God promises as I acknowledge him, I can expect the beauty of his presence. "Let us acknowledge the Lord; let us press on to acknowledge him. As surely as the sun rises, he will appear; he will come to us like the winter rains; like the spring rains that water the earth" (Hos. 6:3, NIV). The words of the prophet Hosea brought a soothing thought and an increased desire to see God appear.

GOD PROMISES AS I ACKNOWLEDGE HIM, I CAN EXPECT THE BEAUTY OF HIS PRESENCE.

Once again, God reminded me he had already begun prepping me through the process of *Love of the Cross* and *Celestial Visions*. Both images came streaming to mind and in that moment I had to decide if I was willing to lay down my life the way Jesus did.

As I stood motionless in silence, I had a sense God's arms were wrapped around me. I was fully aware of his presence. As I stood in silence, giving God my attention, he spoke gently, tenderly, and lovingly into my spirit, "I'm emptying you."

A song by the artist Chris Sligh articulates how I felt that morning and what God meant when he said, *I'm emptying you.* "Empty me of the selfishness inside. Every vain ambition and the poison of my pride. And any foolish thing my heart holds to, Lord empty me of me so I can be filled with You … because everything is a lesser thing, compared to You."

I knew in that moment God had already prepared my heart to surrender my earthly desires and dreams to ensure they were aligned with his. Not that those desires were wrong, but I was now willing to submit to his will above all else.

Emptying was recognizing the need for God to go deeper in and through me. A time to ask God to break down everything that is not pleasing to him. A willingness to lean into the heart of Jesus and embrace him with all my strength. In this moment I knew God wanted to take me somewhere I had never been.

The question that lay before me was this: Am I willing to bear my cross for Jesus or were these only words that I sometimes sang in church? God had readied my heart, so I could willingly surrender as Peter did "so that the tested genuineness of your faith—more precious than gold that perishes though it is tested by fire—may be found to result in praise and glory and honor at the revelation of Jesus Christ" (1 Pet. 1:7, ESV).

God provided everything I needed to take this next step of faith. All I had to provide was my willingness. Isn't this just like my generous God? Always giving so much more than I could ask or imagine.

I stood motionless, tears streaming down my face, transfixed on God's presence. When something is empty, it can then be filled. I wanted to be filled with all of God and I continue to learn that it comes most often by being emptied of me. God can only enter when there is room for him.

I feel that emptying is a willingness to let God do an overhaul in my heart and mind. It's a purging of the soul. Being changed from God is the assurance he will help me be more like him. He will fill me with attributes that are of his character. He is good and the process he chooses to change me will not only be effective, but will always be good for me.

Moses walked away changed after being in the presence of God Almighty. I want to be changed into what God wants me to be. God's intent is always in my best interest. The person I become after God completes a work in me always leaves me more peaceful, more joyful, more thankful, and more certain that I am becoming the best version of me.

In the quietness of my spirit I cried to God saying, "Whatever, Lord, whatever." I knew God was preparing me for a new and unexpected journey, but he had to first possess all of me.

*"When we see him, we shall be like him; for we shall
see him even as he is" (1 John 3:2, NIV).*

Long after God guided me along a path to be emptied and filled with him anew, I came across a similar message by Brother Lawrence. He stated that the heart must be empty of all other things so God can possess the heart alone and do in it what he pleases. Our hearts must be left vacant to him (Lawrence, 2008). It's a matter of giving God my attention and allowing him to live in and through me. He wants me to be an empty *canvas* for God to create a masterpiece.

Surrendering to God's will is never a one-time action because as time goes by and seasons change, so do I. Every year brings a new season of life, whether it's the need to give God a situation to control or the need to ensure my desires align with his. Some years those seasons bring heartache, sometimes the death of a loved one, but comfort comes by relying on God who brings peace, regardless of life's circumstances.

I have to be reminded to focus on God and not myself. I require a conscious effort to come to him empty of self so God can fill me with his desires and what is best for my life. It is trusting and trusting again and day-by-day.

A look back always reveals where God has brought me, evident he was ever-present. Journal entry from 2007: "You may not choose the road ahead, but I chose you." God spoke into my spirit. New beginnings. I love how my life in Christ is guaranteed to have new beginnings.

Walking daily with God is the only way I have the constant awareness of what I need to surrender into his hands. The concerns of life, fretting, questioning, wondering, these are things I hold onto far too long when I lack daily efforts to relinquish my ways of doing things.

I am now in a season of my life that is more unpredictable yet exhilarating because I'm not just saying, "Jesus send me." I'm asking "when?" without knowing where. I have God's beautiful assurance that he and I are walking hand-in-hand where there is nobody else more important than Jesus Christ.

There is a fresh and undeniable measure of God's presence that I have missed out on in times past when I remained in the same pattern and posture during my devotion time. As the weeks passed I committed to standing before God in my kitchen, and slowly I began to understand a greater purpose for being emptied.

Through worship came an intensity for God to occupy all my actions and thoughts. Through the process of yielding, there was a quickening in my spirit and greater appreciation and anticipation for my future when walking with God.

While my eyes were fixated on God and his peace, in what seemed seconds of beginning my worship time, came my *Celestial Vision*.

Emptying became the conduit by which God was able to renew, fill, and strengthen me spiritually, physically, and mentally. Once again God was reminding me of the power that comes from putting my body in a disposition of humility and that this was another way to love him with my entire being.

EMPTYING BECAME THE CONDUIT BY WHICH GOD WAS ABLE TO RENEW, FILL, AND STRENGTHEN ME SPIRITUALLY, PHYSICALLY, AND MENTALLY

In my first book, I shared a dream I called GPS Dream. God lead me up a mountain, showing me how I must be deliberate to follow each step and expect magnificent results.

It is that same determination and direction God wants me to have when it comes to worship. The more I desired to worship the Lord with unwavering devotion, the more confidence I have that he will usher me into his presence. *The more I seek him, the more irresistible he becomes.*

As I presented my heart, mind, body, and soul, and not just through words, God's spirit flowed (2 Tim. 4:5, NLT). I was experiencing an endless flow of God's love. Thankfully, the gift of the Holy Spirit affords me the confidence to know him and recognize his presence and his voice.

It is still a struggle for me to be transparent with other people after years of conditioning in an alcoholic home where I was reminded frequently "don't tell anybody." For me, this is one way God is showing me how I can have radical faith—stepping out boldly for Christ. Radical faith may look different for someone else. It also reveals how God can transform our thinking from years of conditioning that took place as a child.

The more I seek him, the more irresistible he becomes.

Journal entry 1997: "Lord, I know there is something you want to tell me, yet I feel empty. I know I'm unworthy for you to show yourself to me. But, Father, your word promises in Romans 8:26 '… that your spirit intercedes for us …' Lord, search my heart, find any wicked way in me. I desire to pray to where I want to pray more and more! Thank you, Father, for your continued wisdom when I feel lost. You are always there! Lord, you alone are worthy. Thank you for sending Jesus for me so I might live a full life. May the fruits of the Spirit be ever present in my walk with you! Thank you for giving me guidance!" This entry from 1997 reveals how God wants to keep my heart "tuned in" to his. It was also the year of my mother's passing. God is always near.

In 1997, I was telling God I'm not worthy, but in 2016, he chastised me for thinking less of myself. Less of who I am in Christ Jesus. I had to ask for forgiveness because I was basically saying I have no worth, therefore, Christ has no worth in me. God said, "You were unworthy, but when you received my grace and forgiveness, your value, worth, your identity changed. I live in you, therefore, you are of great value, of great worth. You are defined by who you are in Christ Jesus. My grace makes you worthy."

I have the assurance through the Bible the ever-present gift of the Holy Spirit is alive and actively working in my life. Journal entry 1998: "The beauty of walking with God is he is all-knowing. God doesn't allow anything in my life that he has not willingly allowed. He weighs everything going on in my life for my well-being."

By looking back, I can see now that I had no idea what God was preparing for me in the coming months from using my dreams, visions, or his scriptures through simply remaining in him and being a person of prayer.

> *"The man answered, 'You must love the Lord your God with all your heart, all your soul, all your strength, and all your mind'" (Luke 10:27, NLT).*

Part 3

Prayerless Believers

4

Faith-Creating Prayers

"Answered prayers are sometimes the most convincing and faith-creating forces.... If Christians knew how to pray so as to have answers to their prayers, evident, immediate, and demonstrative answers from God, faith would be more widely diffused, would become more general, would be more profound, and would be a much more mighty force in the world" (Bounds, 2000, p. 200).

Randy Clark states there are "unbelieving believers and believing unbelievers" (2011). I would like to add, in order to be a believing believer one cannot be a prayerless believer. Being intentional to know and hear God is built from a foundation of prayer. It's how God begins and continues to stir my heart where I experience "on earth as it is in heaven."

God continues to rearrange my heart for his Spirit to flow freely and expectantly. When I make efforts to protect time to worship God, there's a confidence that the Spirit of God living in me will produce faith-creating prayers. I have an awareness of God's presence and keeping God close to my heart is what produces faith-creating prayers. Faith to ask big!

Without question, receiving answers to prayer has come from an endeavor to be a praying believer. A life absent of prayer clouds my spiritual vision, resulting in a lack of faith simply because I choose on some days to be a prayerless believer.

I WANT TO BE A PRAYING BELIEVER,
NOT A PRAYERLESS BELIEVER.

Until recent days, I must admit the majority of my time in God's presence ended when I got up to go about the routines of my day. God's presence seemed absent, even though I knew I shouldn't live by feelings. On days I didn't "feel" his presence I had no doubt he was with me. However, God has shown me I can experience his tangible presence as a reality and regularly, so I strive to be a prayerful Christian.

God began creating a restlessness in my spirit for "something more precious, more beautiful, more personal," (Lake, 1994, p. xxi). God's presence doesn't have to be sporadic or rare. I can know and sense his tangible presence as he permeates my spirit and heart. I believe he wants me to know him in this way and see his grace at work in my life. This is consistent with his Word.

When I lay my head on my pillow at night and process my day, there is a sense of delight as God's presence has remained with me from the time I walked into the first routines of my day. I have no doubt consistent days in worship, prayer, and reading my Bible is what created an atmosphere in my heart to recognize when God's Spirit was ever-present.

When morning comes and I sit at my table to pick up where I left off the previous morning, immediately his presence hovers. What a thrill! There is urgency in my soul to be with him. Even when I wasn't sitting in a disposition of prayer, this turning point to God's presence stemmed from worship and resulted in a continuous flow of the remarkable Spirit of God flowing through my soul.

The more I worship, I find I don't have to *work* my way into worship. There is a craving in my soul that can only be satisfied in the presence of God. Worship is becoming natural, organic, and there is this peace that is difficult to describe, other than to say I am experiencing a daily walk—hand-in-hand with Jesus—in the same way I experienced from my *Celestial Vision*.

I no longer want to live under the delusion that a little of God results in a continuous flow of his presence and answered prayers. I have no doubt, my previous lack of prayer and worship reduced a ready supply of God's marvelous works and wonders.

Prayers are still answered when I reduce my time with God, nevertheless, a commitment to God by being a praying believer is where he continues to create an atmosphere for me to see him in unexpected ways, which results in multiple miracles. And it changes me in profound ways.

His presence increased in my life and that began by changing my attitude of complacency toward worship and time with God. I did not want to come to God with a nonchalant attitude. If I ever had the opportunity to spend an hour with the Queen of England, I would not go unprepared. How often have I tried to enter God's presence with no preparation and with an attitude of getting it off my checklist, so I could get on with my day?

"Two great truths stand out: where there is much prayer there will be much of the Spirit; where there is much of the Spirit there will be ever-increasing prayer. So clear is the living connection between the two, that when the Spirit is given in answer to prayer it ever wakens more prayer to prepare for the fuller revelation and communication of his Divine power and grace" (Murray, 1898).

If I'm unwilling for God to express himself to me supernaturally, I believe I'm setting God's nature aside and basically accepting what I can see and understand in the natural. I am limited, God is not. Praying is expecting a supernatural reaction and wonderful encounters with God. It is who he is and it is how those strange and unusual experiences are formed. God says, we will "share in his glory," and it's on earth just as it will be when I reach heaven (Rom. 8:17, NLT).

Worship is the gateway into God's presence, and it is where he kindles my entire being to expect his presence in ways I've never asked for or dreamed possible. It's the starting point where he invigorates my soul to believe with unquestionable faith.

When I don't submit to God his way, I'm saddened to think what I miss out on. I am fully confident God has awakened my senses to lead me far away from anything that is boring, typical, and uneventful. God is active, living, exciting, mysterious, and spectacular. I want a vibrant walk with God.

Once again God reminded me, "why would I keep something so glorious hidden from others. Why would I conceal the fullness of his glory?" His love (when embraced) guides us to more faith and belief. I need insight and revelation from my heavenly Father. Am I the only one?

At first, learning to worship God in a variety of ways, beyond words and meditation, brought discomfort because I began doing something different. I've learned that to become comfortable expressing my worship in public (like raising both hands during worship), I must learn to do so in private. It is how God's pushes me to an unquestionable faith and to hear him when I'm least expecting him, in the way my nephew Seth did.

My faith is increasing through making these changes. When Christ ignites a passion in my spirit for more of him, my life is not without his presence or his power. Worship was becoming a lifestyle. A lifestyle where I welcomed and anticipated revelation in the waiting.

"Am I stepping out in faith when things come naturally?" I've been asking myself. I've recognized when it doesn't come easily, naturally, I'm more than likely operating on my own and not relying on the strength of the Lord. I believe obedience in the privacy of my home is giving me the courage to act and react in public when God directs me to do so. To step out beyond my limitations and rely on God's endless creativity brings great rewards.

An example is when people are requesting prayer. It is easy to tell others I am praying for them and I do when I say I will. (At least I try to remember.) It's quick and easy to respond via e-mail, to agree on Facebook, and pray immediately. These are all wonderful ways to ask for help, healing, and comfort; however, most often, stepping out and saying to someone, "can I pray with you right now" doesn't happen. It's uncomfortable.

What I've discovered is when I come to God and expect a moving in my spirit that may be uncomfortable, it is then he teaches me how to love on others through my actions. I want what God is teaching me to help others. I have found hope, peace, and strength many times when someone took a moment to pray with me, not just for me. May God teach all of us to do the same.

Journal entry from 2000, acknowledged my confidence living a Christian life: "I thank the Lord for his presence, his love. I feel foolish to say I can see his blessings coming. I am his child and he has so many blessings to pour out on my family—to bless his church, his work, his workers. I pray for his wisdom and knowledge to take me to a level higher. Christ lives in me, the hope of glory" (Col. 1:27).

Today, I believe I am partaking in those blessings, and God has faithfully taken me to higher levels in his presence because I simply believed him for who he said he is. My road has not been easy. In fact, quite the opposite. However, as my faith grew to expect God's presence in one of his many glorious facets, he repeatedly demonstrated his power with a mighty force.

"And it is impossible to please God without faith. Anyone who wants to come to him must believe that God exists and that he rewards those who sincerely seek him" (Heb. 11:6, NLT). I don't want to be a people pleaser, but I do want to be a God pleaser. Prayer perpetuates a spirit of faith, the confidence to believe in what I don't see. And prayer equips me to step forward into what is uncertain. Prayer is planting a seed. It's the seed where I experience and expect miracles to unfold and blossom. Prayer gives God something to *water*.

Prayer opens me up to be filled with the Spirit. The Spirit helps me recognize my need for more of God. My prayer invites God to abide in me with freedom. Remaining spirit-filled fosters a need for more of God. A freedom in the Spirit where there is "nothing between us and God, our faces shining with the brightness of his face. And so we are transfigured much like the Messiah, our lives gradually becoming brighter and more beautiful as God enters our lives and we become like him" (2 Cor. 3:17, MSG). This freedom in the Spirit creates in me a God-centered, God-directed life.

I have no doubt a one-sentence prayer, a five minute devotion, can move the hand of God. However, *a clear and unmistakable word from the Lord* has come most often from a determination and intentionality for Christ to occupy my mind, body, and soul. There is only one word required to describe how to get to this point—time. Time with God is essential to knowing and receiving insight and revelation from him regularly.

As for me, God has different work for each of us, and we must seek him in this matter. God is teaching me to look at prayer as my job and that is where and how I have seen progress and grow deeper in the knowledge and love of God in the spiritual realm. It's the *how* God helps me to have "the mind of Christ." At first I felt ridiculous stating "prayer and worship are my job." However, since God began impressing this upon my heart and after I journaled this directive from the Lord, I've read several resources and teachers of the gospel who have stated the same of their lives. It has also been confirmed to me by godly people in my life. God employs me to be a praying believer.

I think the biggest barrier to spending time with God is saying yes to people and events and saying no to God. At first it doesn't look like I'm saying no to God, but when I'm too busy to spend time with him, I'm guilty of doing exactly that. I don't want to let other people down, but how often do I let God down? At times, I let others down, but the reality is I let God down far more often.

Torrey, Brother Lawrence, John Lake, Bill Johnson, and others have reiterated there is no presence more satisfying than God's presence. It is a beautiful thing to walk with a consciousness that God is always present. God's presence doesn't have to be fleeting and it won't be when my time with him isn't fleeting.

God not only confirmed that worship was my daily priority through other Christian resources, but one night during a service with guest speaker Todd White as well. The service was entirely focused on healing. I have many chronic conditions (epilepsy, colitis, and thyroid disease) and was eager to be prayed over. No matter how many times I have been prayed for in the past and not yet seen a change, I still believe that there will come a day that God heals me completely. I went up to the altar with the same expectation. "Lord, I want to hear you and I want your healing touch. The way your blood was shed, may your blood bring total healing."

What I was seeking and what resulted were two different things. A woman I do not know and who did not know me, began to pray over me. First, for a moment she stood in silence and then said "you're a worshipper, you raise your hands, you give God your entire being. He wants you to stop going about your day with routines and "busy work." Your day is to be filled in his presence and worship him."

I was overwhelmed by God's love because this unknown woman validated what God had already been impressing on my spirit. To worship the Lord in spirit and soul and body (1 Thess. 5:23, NLT).

I later chuckled at how I went up to be prayed over for healing, but God had an entirely different message for me. My request for healing was secondary to the message God had for me at that specific time in my life. God was reminding me, "Listen to me, worship me, and do what I tell you. Stop questioning."

I believe healing will follow as my focus remains on God and his ways, not mine. What I've learned in the months following is by exercising a spirit of worship, God develops in me a spirit to believe, not only in my own healing, but that of others. As the saying goes, "I can't give away what I don't have." My focus and love for God also instills trust to wait patiently on God's timing.

After the conference and taking time on my own to listen and acknowledge him the way he had reminded me, he spoke into my spirit when I was alone. "Your job is to worship, your time is to be my time." I walked away from this confirmation with great joy and a confidence that God himself had defined how my time should be spent. This work for him was now "my job." My husband goes to work on a train. I go to work on my knees.

I've come to realize that understanding this commitment to God as a "job," is the only way he has been able to get through to me the importance of not neglecting worship and prayer with him.

In the following weeks, I began to see that an active time of worship is where God can begin to increase my faith to step into the impossible. God knows I need this; therefore, I embraced calling this "my job," knowing that many people will snicker or even disapprove of how I spend my time. This is when I must stand on the solid ground of scripture to please God and not man.

When I would say *no*, to others I bore this constant guilt of letting people down. In the course of a year, as I let God invade my mind and actions, he repeatedly said, "Let your yes be yes, and your no be no" (James 5:12). I need not offer any explanation when God says to do something. God is teaching me to let my yes be yes, and no be no. It doesn't come easily.

Though many of my routines and *yeses* to people are good, I must let the Lord guide all my steps. God was showing me when I always say *yes* to people, I take away the blessing God had prepared for someone else to step into. The thought of this gave me strength to let go of my way of doing things so God could let others do his will and be blessed.

It's a blessed season of life with more time to commit to the Lord regularly and with more energy. My husband and I are now "empty-nesters." Our two sons are living independent lives, both married. Relinquishing my professional career for God's calling on my life affords me more time to do what God has called me to. I have the privilege and blessing to write as God directs me in the comforts of my home.

What God continues to show me is that busy work keeps me from knowing him. "Busy work" is what can keep me from being active in my work for the Kingdom of God. It is still a struggle and doesn't come easy to say no to others. Nevertheless, I've asked God to help me recognize when I am saying no to him.

I look forward to the day when I can more readily discern God's direction because I'm walking continually in his presence. Walking in

God's Spirit is what gives insight, so I don't do my own thing but God's *thing*. And the more I practice this, the more they become the same.

> *"Prayer does not stand alone. It is not an isolated performance. Prayer stands in closest connection with all the duties of an ardent piety. It is the issuance of a character which is made up of the elements of a vigorous and commanding faith. Prayer honors God, acknowledges his being, exalts his power, adores his providence, secures his aid" (Bounds, 2000, p. 338).*

Over the years, I would do a quick evaluation of the hours I spent at work, attending my children's activities, time in ministry and other family responsibilities. No matter the season, many hours have been and are wasted on me and less for God. Every book I read, whether from the sixteenth or twenty-first centuries have a common theme—the church is too busy to pray, to gather in worship with other believers, and do the work of the Lord.

My friend and I were having a conversation about human nature and how it is not different for us now than it was for those who lived centuries ago. She added that the difference today is our lives are more complex.

With modern technology, we can do more at a faster pace, and it's one reason we are easily distracted from the things of God. We constantly sit on our computers, phones, television, with our hands and minds connecting to a stream of information, much of it excessive and trivial.

Before gas operated farm equipment, many used the excuse they couldn't meet weekly with a community of believers, because of the need to be up before sunrise and work until sunset. They were too tired to spend time in prayer. Yet at that same time, there were those with such a great hunger for God they walked ten miles or more to hear the Word of God.

I am thankful I live in a country and time in history where I don't have to walk ten miles to hear the Word of God. With my podcast app I can listen to sermons from all over the world while I walk for pleasure. In times past life was different, but century after century the Church has the same excuse—too busy to pray because there is too much to do. We do what we want to do. So why don't we start being honest with ourselves and everyone around us and just say, "It's not a priority of mine to spend time with God."

I imagine many of us have been caught in the trap of distraction and too often we blame the devil for being too busy in our chaotic world. However, *the trap is not being too busy, the trap is that we accept his lie.* There's always a sufficient amount of time in a day to be with God. It's time to stop giving Satan credit for the choices we make.

Comparing my life to the lifestyle of those in centuries past, I came to the realization I wasn't willing to allow God to change my lifestyle in his way. I was operating with God my way. It wasn't my intention, but there is no doubt information overload kept me from recognizing God in my surroundings.

In many ways, carrying on with the responsibilities in life gave me the illusion I was doing more than enough for God. Doing something for God didn't mean I needed to do more. Because I chose the majority of my schedule, in my mind I was doing enough for God. I don't want "just enough of God." I want all of God.

If I want something badly enough, I can make it happen and will do what is necessary to achieve it. Do I want God more than anything? Do I want to receive revelation more than any other information? The answer is *yes!* Therefore, I best be clear about how I spend the limited hours in each day. I must choose God first every day.

Finding ten or fifteen minutes a day to be with God is the easy part. It's in the waiting that takes more time and effort. We can't continue living under the illusion that a little of God is transformational. I believe change comes when worship becomes a way of life.

The primary feedback I received from my first book was how people realized they needed to return to a more consistent time of prayer and reading the Bible. Commonly, we all want to meet the minimum requirement. I have a natural tendency to give God less of my time, which is illogical when there are great revelations and beautiful moments during times of worship and prayer. But I have come to understand it is the result of our flesh, our nature.

God knows I cannot do anything without his Spirit enabling me, especially in the twenty-first century, where our lives are more complex, and our souls are crushed by the weight of information and the frenzy of the marketplace. "For the flesh desires what is contrary to the Spirit, and the Spirit what is contrary to the flesh" (Gal. 5:17, NIV).

The more I commit to meaningful time with God, the more I reduce the danger of having a superficial knowledge of and relationship with Christ. I want, and more importantly, God wants my time with him to have substance, depth in heart, body, mind, and soul which creates depth in relationship.

God wants to be the driving force and voice in my life. God will make his majestic voice known. Isa. 30:30

I want to be a praying believer, to see God, and walk expectantly, hand-in-hand, and give him permission to manifest himself for what he knows I need for each day, for his glory. He is a personal God and our relationship is specific. Indeed the very hairs on my head are numbered (Luke 12:7). I will boast continually of God's glorious presence. I have nothing to hide when it comes to my love for God.

"Aren't you looking for signs and wonders, manifestation from God?" some ask. The word *manifest* turns Christians off, however, I am not ashamed to say I look for God to display his glory! I need spiritual revelation, God's insight, and wisdom. I want God, all of him, and I don't want him to pass me by. I don't want to dictate, define, or quench the Spirit of God coming in all his fullness. Life with God is such a glorious adventure.

I will not submit to man's limitations about how God *should* operate. I don't want to rule out the supernatural aspects of God, which appear beyond my reach or imagination living in Christ. To do so, would be to diminish God's sovereignty. To omit the word *manifest* from my vocabulary is reducing God to what is natural, limited, everything God is not. God is supernatural.

*"Christians are wasting their lives in the terrible bondage
of the world instead of living in the manifestation and the
privilege and the glory of the child of God" (Murray, 1953).*

The beauty of God's presence is he came to me as a child when I had no prior knowledge of the different ways he speaks. What I did know is I could talk to him and it was from this blind-faith he visited me with a vision. A. B. Simpson states that "when we can see, it is not faith but reasoning" (iBooks file).

Visions of Uncertainty

At the time God gave me my first vision, I had never heard a sermon or testimony where God spoke to someone through dreams and visions. I did know, however, that God's word says that when we are children of God, we are led by his Spirit (Rom. 8:14).

I knew God, I needed him, and he had a specific message for me at a time when I needed guidance of some kind. When I didn't know and understand who God was and how he spoke, he came to me. God knew I needed something in order to not give up on the challenges I was experiencing in my home.

My father was an alcoholic, and it was alcohol that so often created turmoil and unrest in our home, both physically and mentally. Regardless, I honored, respected, and thanked God for the love my father had for my family and me. I loved him dearly; he was my father after all.

Twenty-one years of living with my parents included long days and nights, fearing my father's return home in a drunken rage. However, my father was a completely different person when he was sober. His demeanor was calming. He was patient, quick to listen, slow to speak.

My father did not cry unless he was intoxicated. Drunk, his emotions were reduced to sorrow, anger, rage, empathy. Alcohol made him unpredictable and that is often the scariest thing a child can live with.

Despite his disease of alcoholism, he was a great man. When he was sober I cannot recall a time when he yelled, lashed out with contempt, or created an environment of mental abuse. He was loving, patient, and provided a welcoming atmosphere to everyone. He knew how to have a good time, regularly played pranks, and we often heard, "everyone loves your dad." These were sincere and genuine views of my father.

My father was generous and continually gave of his possessions to those in need. His kitchen was your kitchen and his food was your food. If you were around when the grill was going, you could count on being invited to dinner. It didn't matter who you were, family or guest, you were never given scraps. The best was always served, and he continually made sure there was enough for seconds.

There were those who took advantage of his generosity, and though he knew it, he always responded, "They're not bothering anybody." He'd leave it at that and so would the rest of us. Gossip and negativity were never tolerated.

Because the behavior of an alcoholic is unpredictable we relished the evenings and weekends of being together, laughing, playing games and cards when alcohol wasn't the beverage for the night.

Living with an alcoholic created this continual desire to get out of the environment, to be relieved of the anxiousness that always pervaded the home and my heart. As the years went by, challenges and circumstances, though different, continued to escalate, I never gave up hope. Hope that my father would allow Christ to save him from this destructiveness. Hope for a better day.

The Bible describes hope as those things we cannot see, therefore, I ended each year with the hope it would be the year of his salvation. Years went by with the same prayer, for God to deliver his soul and that his drinking would cease. It seemed but a dream—an impossibility.

As the stress and heartache from a broken home increased through my teen years, I found myself hating my life, wanting to escape. I didn't have the confidence to go anywhere else, and it was during this time that I had my first vision. A vision was something I had never heard of before. Just like my *Celestial Vision*, no explanation of what was happening was necessary. When God is present, there is no doubt.

Today, I am blessed by my past because of God's grace and faithfulness to bring me through many storms. His love was unfailing to the end during each season of pain. A life of perseverance is how God enlarged my future and hope for what I did not see. "Hope is more than a desire to change things, it is expecting better is coming," I would tell myself.

Though young, I found myself praying throughout the day, long into the evening. These were the times I felt God's presence for the first time and even in my ignorance of God, I was a prayerful believer. I was desperate to know I wasn't alone. It was during these years spending time with God in isolation, he refreshed my soul through an encounter of his presence.

It was from my desperation as a child that God came to me when I wasn't looking for him. He provided what I needed for the present and gave me a promise I held onto for years. It's what I call my *Campfire Vision*.

"… In some secret house hiding from authorities, or in Simon's house on a street called Straight—they prayed! In the morning and sometimes all night, they prayed without ceasing. Cornelius prayed always and Peter prayed on rooftops. By the seashore, in the temple, or in the desert, they called upon the Lord continually. They spent hours and days shut in with God, until they received clear, detailed guidance. And what incredible specifics God gave them" (David Wilkerson Today, World Challenge, September 3, 2014).

Campfire Vision

I was standing by a campfire and the logs were burning, the flames rising higher and higher. The Spirit of God said "the fire is intense, your trials will increase, but one day there will be nothing left but smoke, residue. As the fires increase, I am with you."

End of vision

It wasn't the vision I would have asked for, but God is a God of peace and immediately I had a sense of hope and assurance. I didn't enjoy hearing "as the fires increase," indicating I would experience more difficulties ahead. However, what nourished my soul immediately was a sense of calm. My focus automatically went to the beauty of God's presence and nature. Peace.

Though I had no idea what the future would hold, the Lord was preparing me for multiple trials. It's hard to explain, but when God impresses a message (including one you would not choose to receive), there is a sense of tranquility things will come together. He was leading as long as I was willing to follow. I had no doubt God would stand by his Word.

As I learned to wait upon the Lord, God taught me how moments with him are opportunities to see as he sees. Moses asked God to see his glory. God expressed what he meant in Exodus 33:18–19a: "And the Lord said 'I will cause all my goodness to pass in front of you, and I will proclaim my name, the Lord, in your presence'" (NIV). When God passes by, I do not want to miss him.

As a youth, though I knew little of God's character, my vision had this sense of a "father daughter" conversation. It was simple yet supernatural.

When the trials and fires of life intensified, as God told me they would, I reflected on this vision many times. I prayed, pleaded, and asked God to step in and remove me from the heat. Instead, it was as though the flames were ignited, rising higher and higher.

My father's poor choices, which were outside the will of God, kept me praying. When things looked as though they could not get worse, they did. The more I talked with God, the more he increased my understanding of the devil's unseen forces at work. Spiritual warfare continued raging and the enemy hovered continually, trying to rip away my joy and my father's soul.

Life with my father was never meant to be a continual spiritual battle. Unfortunately, my father used his free will to choose poorly and naturally this affected those around him for decades.

A few years later, though I don't quite recall the time frame, God once again caught my attention when I didn't expect it. I had my second vision, which I call the *Rocky Road Vision*. As before, I wasn't looking for God to speak in this way. God was once again stepping in, reminding me he is always with me.

When God reveals insight to the meaning of dreams and visions I can't think of a time when he didn't validate them through the Scripture or another dream. *Relying on God's Word is critical to hearing his voice clearly.* When God steps in and speaks, it is undeniably him, and what invades my mind and spirit is his divine love.

Rocky Road Vision

I was walking down a muddy, unpaved road. The path was uneven, filled with potholes, rocks, too many to avoid. Jesus was in front, in white, holding my hand as he led me along. I wanted to avoid the mud at all costs, but we didn't steer clear dredging through mud and potholes. I didn't want to sink. The terrain was the same the entire vision. Through the rocks, uneven path, continuing to walk step-in-step with Christ. As long as I followed, my feet never turned. My feelings in the vision were calm, peace. At no time was I anxious, but simply following. Jesus said, "Your road is rough, it will be rough, but I am with you. Take my hand, follow me, follow in my footsteps, I am with you."

End of vision

I never saw Christ's face, but the words I heard once again sustained me for years to come. I longed for visions with white doves, but that was not my path. Life wasn't going to get easier anytime soon.

Though the roads were rocky and unpaved, this was a constant reminder I was never alone. The terrain representing life's challenges were difficult for several decades, but the Lord was always present, walking before me, just as he promised in his word and revealed to me through my visions.

I recall stating later how the road was rocky, and I had moments I thought I would never see "paved roads" again. One of the beautiful promises complimenting this vision came from one of my favorite chapters in the Bible. In the book of 2 Samuel there is a beautiful song written by King David.

David's beautiful song of praise gave life to my visions to press on with hope. "… As for God, his way is perfect. All the Lord's promises prove true … he has made my way safe. You have made a wide path for my feet to keep them from slipping (2 Samuel 22, NLT). Another version states my "ankles will not turn." (*Rocky Road Vision*)

Just as God had warned, the roads became more difficult, with what seemed to be continual setbacks from the goal of seeing my father saved. Two decades after receiving these visions, the Lord gave a sequel to both visions.

These first two visions comforted me for over two decades with a continual assurance God was and would always be with me. God lead the way, and it was his faithfulness and grace that sustained me.

God continues to write my story, my God-story, and one of the chapters along life's journey was what I call *Campfire Vision Updated.* I saw this vision "in the waiting."

"Meanwhile, the moment we get tired in the waiting, God's Spirit is right alongside helping us along. If we don't know how or what to pray, it doesn't matter. He does our praying in and for us, making prayer out of our wordless sighs, our aching groans. He knows us far better than we know ourselves … and keeps us present before God. That's why we can be so sure that every detail in our lives of love for God is worked into something good (Rom. 8:26–28, MSG).

Campfire Vision Updated

It was the same campfire, but this time what remained were smoke and embers, flames no longer rising to the sky. God simply said, "One day the fire will die down, the embers will cease, the smoke is only the residue of what was. One day the fire will go out."

End of vision

Once again, I would have preferred an immediate glimpse of white, fluffy clouds, doves, and rainbows, but I knew God was preparing, equipping, and giving me what I needed to sustain me in the present and for the future. I was given hope to keep following and trusting God. The Lord graciously nourished my soul, even though I wished "one day" would be "now."

After my mother's passing, circumstances surrounding my father's decisions effected our family in greater ways. These three visions became specific prayer requests, even though I had received them more than two decades prior. God reminded me of these visions and though they appeared alarming, they brought peace because God showed me he was my protector.

One Saturday, during some very trying times, God lead me to the verse in Exodus 13:12, when the Israelites wandered in the desert. God provided a cloud by day to protect them from the heat and provided a fire by night to protect them from the cold. The very next morning at church, the pastor received a word from the Lord, read this exact passage aloud, then said, "These verses are for someone here today." I saw God work supernaturally through others, for my well-being, and in the simplest, most straightforward ways.

The situations didn't change, but when God revealed his presence and how he was hovering over me, there was a calm, a peace that is unexplainable. This passage of scripture gave me the confidence to stand up that morning and go about my day, knowing God saw everything and was my protector and guide.

We often had bonfires in our backyard, and my husband would burn several pallets at once. The more pallets, the greater the fire and intensity of the heat. No matter how many pallets were burned or how high the flames shot up to the sky, if we wanted the fire to keep going, we had to throw more wood on the fire. These times were for our enjoyment, but they also produced heat and comfort on cold Michigan evenings.

In order to obtain the full warmth of a bonfire, I had to remain close enough to feel the heat. These visions were symbolic reminders how God desires to *kindle* my heart to receive the hope of his protection and safety, but I must be near him to sense his presence.

In the *Campfire Vision,* there was no figure of Jesus, just his gentle words, which confirmed his presence. I knew God was present though I couldn't see him. The second dream that followed, *Rocky Road Vision*, I could see how Jesus was leading and hearing his instructions to keep following.

Only God can fan the flames in my spirit, especially when there is an intensity to the flames of life. Being refueled by the Holy Spirit cannot take place without being a praying believer and reading the Bible. They were beautiful promises as a way to increase my faith regardless of my life's circumstances. An assurance God was not only leading and a reminder to enjoy the calm, warm glow of his presence in the process. And restored confidence in God in the present because he loved me enough to give me some detail for the future.

God never failed me. Not once, and he never will! Deut. 31:8

5

Adventures in Immersion

"God is not silent. It is the nature of God to speak. The second person of the Holy Trinity is called, 'The Word'" (Tozer, 2009, p. 54).

God continued to sketch into my mind and heart a greater understanding of how to gaze upon his glory and visualize how he operates from heaven to earth. A pattern was forming with a central message of the Gospel, derived from *Love of the Cross* and *Celestial Visions*. God had my attention.

Increased revelation came through silence and sitting in God's presence. When God created the heavens and the earth, there was silence. There was a void, nothing. In God's perfect timing he spoke and created something out of nothing. I find the same to be true about how he speaks and teaches. It is when I purposefully quiet my soul, sit in silence and wait on God, he most often steps in and speaks life from nothing.

I began to see how these visions could be applied to my prayer life and a way in which to be escorted to the feet of Jesus. Worshipping God for who he is and what he did opened my spirit and effortless worship was birthed. These visions became the foundation for lavishing God with the praise he deserves and entering into his presence.

Every time God speaks and his presence is tangible, I believe it is a miracle. God rendered me speechless and the adventures with God continue and the miracles have just begun.

"He [Jesus] was taken back up to heaven where he sat down at the right side of God" (John 16:19, MSG).

Parachute Dream

I jumped out of a plane with three people. One was Kirk Douglas, the movie star, and his son, Michael Douglas. There was no face to the third parachuter. As we hung in the sky, Kirk Douglas took his parachute and engulfed me inside his parachute. Michael Douglas did the same, and then the third to where we were all enveloped together.
End of dream

Interpretation of Parachute Dream

The interpretation was quite simple. Three in One Father (Kurt Douglas), Son (Michael Douglas), and the Holy Spirit (no face, invisible). The Trinity, three-in-one, protecting, keeping me "under their wings." A beautiful adventure with God, being immersed in his presence.

Jesus often spoke in parables and metaphors. I find it no different today if I am looking and expecting. The order of my dreams and visions, starting with the *Cross Vision*, became chapters in my God-story. The *Parachute Dream* was a delightful addition about how God holds me close to his heart, protects, and covers me with his love.

The Lord is teaching me to recognize there is importance to the order in which he speaks, whether through the Word, sermons, dreams, or visions. When I looked at this dream, together with those mentioned in previous chapters, a beautiful, simplified summary of the Gospel of Jesus Christ was revealed. Though each dream was different, they all pointed to God's heavenliness and the mystery of the Trinity.

God doesn't set up perimeters about how to pray, but these "pictures" provided insight how to enhance my prayers by having greater insight into God, who is Three in One.

My *Parachute Dream* beautifully portrays the Trinity—the Father, Son, and Holy Spirit—working as one. Three in the Bible represents divine fullness, triumph as was the case when Jesus was buried and rose from the dead on the third day.

I'm not a risk-taker by nature, but I've discovered, through God's help, there is a greater degree of joy by stepping out and trusting him. God gave me a beautiful picture how he surrounds me and shrouds me in his love.

God did more than set my imagination on fire. He opened my eyes to see how the radiance of heaven is Three in One.

When I wrote my first book, it felt like a big risk. I can honestly say this second time around, taking another risk in obedience to God's instructions, is fun and exhilarating. I want to expect nothing less. I don't want to be a boring and lifeless believer.

I want to see God in all his might and glory and for others to have their own experiences that are thrilling and exciting—not for the sake of a thrill but to see others share in the love for God because he is God and to know what a thrill it is to love God! So many things in life are thrilling and shouldn't we experience how God is the most thrilling of all?

The fulfillment of Christ's divine purpose was completed through the resurrection granting me his presence that stays with me through the working of the Holy Spirit. The Bible also refers to the Holy Spirit as my Comforter (John 14:16). His presence continually goes with me, and what a privilege to know I am wrapped in God's love and embrace.

"… We must continuously walk in God's Spirit, since in the spirit-life not to advance is to fall back. But those who have the wind of the Holy Spirit in their souls glide ahead even while they sleep … The more I spent with God, the more I wanted to know him, and the more I wanted to know him, I discovered him, and God began to sculpt my soul and heart raised up into God's presence" (Lawrence, 2008).

The significance and operation of the Trinity was how God immersed, covered, and lavished me to take the mysterious part of his nature into daily, practical application and action, resulting in faith-creating prayers.

*"… With Christ, who gives us the best picture of
God we'll ever get (2 Cor. 4:4, MSG).*

Time with God is anything but ordinary, and the more I worshipped, the less structured it felt, unlike times past when time with God may have felt mundane or constructed.

Think of my *parachute dream*. Just like parachuting is adventurous and exhilarating in its own way, so became my time with God. I had this beautiful picture of how fun God is and the joy of soaring along in and with him. Every day brought a new excitement to be swooped up by God, gliding along, carried by his loving presence.

With this understanding, I looked back and pondered previous chapters from the *Love of the Cross* and *Celestial Visions*. Combined, I had a story to tell, a story to proclaim, another God-story to profess as my own.

To remain in Christ, I have to first jump and allow him to catch me. It's then I am resting and soaring where he leads. He is a God of relationship and he longs to be with us. I had this wonderful sense of God's gentle voice, "Come to me, stay with me."

*"… Cry[ing] out to God in the secret place and taking
risks in the public place" (Clark, 2011).*

God's Throne Room Vision

Shortly thereafter, it was another morning in my kitchen, which has become my "altar" and where I spend my alone time with God. God quietly spoke into my spirit to stand in silence. This directive from the Lord has truly become his way to humble me.

There's such joy knowing God is available and has time for me. I do not want my pride getting in the way of standing before him in the privacy of my own home because it sounds weird. Life is simply not about me, but God, always. These simple gestures have kept my time with God fresh and new.

Recognizing and acknowledging God's sovereignty during these times continue to create delightful moments, and it is how he ushers me into his awe-inspiring presence. There's no mistaking something is happening supernaturally. I believe God's grace and presence is meant to be perpetual.

God reminded me to expect heaven to open, and I was purposeful to keep my mind from wandering away from God. "The promise of open heavens is conditional: 'The Lord will open the heavens … if you pay attention to the commands of the Lord your God …'" (Deut. 28:12–13, NIV). "Love the Lord your God with all your heart and with all your soul and with all your mind and with all your strength" (Mark 12:30, NIV). Being under an open heaven, above all else, is a love relationship" (Orton, 2014).

A vision appeared, and I began to see God sitting solemnly on his throne. No face, but a form that I understood to be the supreme, Living God. I wasn't sure what it meant for God to be solemn. It wouldn't be for several months until I understood why I was seeing God sitting solemnly on his throne and what this meant.

It was another moment, where the beauty of God was unmistakable. In the book of Revelation, God opened John's eyes to see heaven open in the spiritual realm that he could not see in the natural.

In Revelation 4:1–2, in the J. B. Phillips New Testament (Phillips), John wrote, "Later I looked again, and before my eyes a door stood open in heaven, and in my ears was the voice with the ring of a trumpet, which I had heard at first, speaking to me and saying, 'Come up here, and I will show you what must happen in the future.' Immediately I knew myself to be inspired by the Spirit, and in my vision I saw a throne had been set up in heaven, and there was someone seated upon the throne."

These verses give me goosebumps. I can feel the spirit of God flowing through me like a fresh stream down his holy mountain.

A few days later, I had the same image before me, but this time I had a glimpse of Jesus sitting, facing God. They were conversing and gently, Christ was making my requests known to God the Father. Before me was a beautiful peek of the Father-Son relationship and how I am at the center of God's thoughts.

> *"And the Father who knows all hearts knows what the Spirit is saying, for the Spirit pleads for us believers in harmony with God's own will" (Rom. 8:27, NLT).*

The Bible states everything Jesus does must come from the will of the Father. As God reveals his will for my life to the Son, it is for the purpose the Son will be glorified and in turn the Father will be glorified.

> *"Jesus said these things. Then, raising his eyes in prayer, he said: Father, it's time. Display the bright splendor of your Son so the Son in turn may show your bright splendor. You put him in charge of everything human so he might give real and eternal life to all in his charge. And this is the real and eternal life: That they know you, the one and only true God, And Jesus Christ, whom you sent. I glorified you on earth by completing down to the last detail what you assigned me to do. And now, Father, glorify me with your very own splendor, the very splendor I had in your presence before there was a world" (John 17:1–5, MSG).*

Standing before God opened my heart and eyes to keep before me the illustration of the Three working as One. Each revelation was a thrilling climax to his story and God's Word, validating and bringing life to all. The "story" looking like an instruction manual reinforcing the order and importance of how God defines the Father, Son, and the Holy Spirit.

How I prayed verbally and physically changed that morning. I stood in my kitchen, raised my hands toward the heavens, and thanked God how he controls all things, and his plans are perfectly orchestrated. I thanked God for the promise "from the moment we began praying" (Dan. 9:23, NLT), and Jesus began interceding on my behalf.

For a brief moment, I thought if someone were looking in my window they would see how ridiculous I looked. As I try to convey this, it sounds ridiculous, even comical. Was it necessary to move my body into action? I believe it was, primarily out of obedience to God. But also one example of how God continued to provide a plentiful supply of his presence.

There is something about uninhibited worship, presenting to God my entire being, giving permission for the Holy Spirit to engulf and empower me to walk in him. Praise that is visible and vocal is powerful.

When he asks me to jump, take risks, I can count on the fact he shrouds, protects, (*Parachute Dream*) and takes me to heights I never would have gone. Without a willingness to look ridiculous I may have missed God ushering me into his presence anew.

Obedience breeds blessings, and God simply wanted me to stand. A vibrant, active prayer life comes from a willingness to be vulnerable. Vulnerable not only being transparent with others, but taking risk so my vulnerability turns into victory. A vibrant prayer life breeds vulnerability and vulnerability breeds victory.

Vibrancy = Vulnerability = Victory

In the following days, standing in my kitchen, worshipping God, I continued to see the image of God sitting solemnly on his throne. My first reaction was the same as when I saw Jesus on the Cross. I acknowledged his Majesty, his Beauty, his Kingdom and stood before him reverently the way I would an earthy king.

The Lord revealed how I could have a hands-on relationship because of his hand on my life. Weaved within this passage in John is a beautiful illustration of the Father, Three in One. God's revelation validating and summing up these three scenes (*Love of the Cross* and *Celestial Visions,* and *Parachute Dream*) and what is central to the faith of a Christian.

It wouldn't be for several months until God brought revelation to this vision and gave me the answer to my question, "what does it mean when God sits solemnly on his throne?"

"… The goal is for all of them to become one heart and mind—
Just as you, Father, are in me and I in you, so they might be one
heart and mind with us (Parachute Dream). Then the world might
believe that you, in fact, sent me. The same glory you gave me, I
gave them, So they'll be as unified and together as we are—
I in them and you in me.
Then they'll be mature in this oneness,
And give the godless world evidence
That you've sent me and loved them
In the same way you've loved me. (Love of the Cross)
Father, I want those you gave me, to be with me, right where I am,
So they can see my glory, the splendor you gave me (Celestial Vision),
Having loved me" (John 17, MSG).

Part 4

Unquenchable Fire

6

His Fire Burns

"No, the wisdom we speak of is the mystery of God ... For his Spirit ... shows us God's deepest secrets ... using the Spirit's words to explain spiritual truths" (1 Cor. 2:7–13, NLT).

Burning Heart of God

The days I spent obediently worshipping God was how he created within me an inner sensitivity and an awakening of my senses to his supreme being. I'm continually amazed at God's willingness to reveal his heart in unfamiliar ways.

I don't want to squelch the heart of God in me. To do so would be to dismiss his plans for my life. Had I done so, I would not have experienced what was next, the burning heart of God.

In the quiet place of my heart and home, God came down and taught me something new, again. God continued to impress upon me the importance of not burying details of his great power and wonders within my journals. "Reveal what and how I'm teaching you," he continued speaking into my spirit. He gave me yet another encounter to boast in him.

These frequent experiences with God did not come from short intervals where prayers were on auto-pilot. When my praise and worship was fresh each day, there became an instinctive reaction to respond to the moving of the Holy Spirit. *More time with God is, without question, richer.*

I have found and continue to find that when I take the initiative to live in the presence of God, education and theological knowledge is secondary to being taught firsthand by God. What I lack in knowledge from man does not hinder seeing and receiving to see God anew. If I don't look to God as the unchanging, divine being, I would not have been confronted by the Person, Jesus Christ.

At the end of the Lord's Prayer in *The Message* translation of the Bible, Jesus calls out the supremacy of God: "You're in charge! You can do anything you want! You're ablaze in beauty!" (Matt. 6:13).

It was a Sunday morning service and the congregation was singing praises to God. My eyes were fixed on God as we sung; my focus was single-minded toward the heavens, not on myself. The pastor asked us to stand for prayer.

The supernatural presence of God, the Holy Spirit, hovered over me and presented himself in a way I had never experienced previously. It was sudden and God began doing something extraordinary.

As the congregation stood, the pastor asked us to pray for a missionary who was being held captive for sharing the Gospel of Christ in a Muslim nation. He was awaiting execution by beheading, willing to be a martyr for Christ.

The congregation took a moment to pray, asking God to intervene and deliver him from persecution. As we stood in silence, each interceding in their own way, my eyes began to burn like fire. This wasn't a vision but a moment when one of my five senses was being awakened from the heart of God. Something tangible was taking place so I stood completely still, unsure what else to do. It's a phenomenon of the Spirit of God that can't be explained.

Instantly, in the quietness of my spirit, I felt and heard the heart of God, "The way your eyes burn like fire is the pain of my heart." I couldn't move if I wanted to. "Our God is a consuming fire" (Heb. 12:29, NIV).

Though God's fire was burning in my heart, I felt the love and gentleness of his voice. Slowly, tears streamed down my face. God's presence was so gripping I didn't move to wipe away the tears. I wanted to feel the heart of God, and the stinging in my eyes kept me focused on his heart, not mine. I didn't want to ignore his communication to me.

His love is infinite, and it was a moment when God revealed to me what he sees, feels, heart-to-heart as though I was with my best friend, sharing something so personal and intimate. God revealed his love through an unexplainable, "unquenchable fire"; the Holy Spirit's fire.

"Our opportunities for serving him will spring out of our knowledge of him; he will see to that. The Lord, the Spirit is arranging his own work. He knows where need exists, and when he sees someone who can meet that need he can make contact" (Sparks, 2000, p. 119).

I began to have a greater understanding why God must empty me. As I have the desire to let God enlarge his presence in my life, I find my thoughts aren't clouded, preventing me from seeing as God wants me to see. It is another opportunity for me to be used by God.

Shortly after this experience and praying for God's children, the news began reporting mass killings of Christians. This experience, I believe, is God's way of reminding me to not neglect the importance to pray for those being persecuted for being a Christ follower. God instructs us through his word to be "praying for all the saints," God's dedicated servants (Eph. 6).

"Do you see what we've got? An unshakable kingdom! And do you see how thankful we must be? Not only thankful, but brimming with worship, deeply reverent before God. For God is not an indifferent bystander. He's actively cleaning house, torching all that needs to burn, and he won't quit until it's all cleansed. God himself is Fire!" (Heb. 12:28–29, MSG).

Heart and Eyes Burn Like Fire—Again

"A fire comes to a person's soul when that believer is filled with the Spirit, and there comes a passionate burning to know Christ and to share his gospel. An ignited person with an ignited heart is the one baptized by the Spirit's fire" (Kinlaw, 2002, p. 81).

Several months later, I had just finished reading my Bible and placed my head on the table to sit in God's presence. As I sat in silence, my eyes began to burn like fire the same way I experienced previously in church. There was a quickening and intensity of burning, a tangible fire sensation in my eyes. As before, I knew it was God connecting my heart to his.

God stepped in, and I was receiving a glimpse of the heavenly realm. God was identifiable and there was no mistaking his presence. It began when I started praying for my children. God's love for my children is much greater than my love for them. This is hard to grasp for there is nothing more in this world than the love I have for my family.

God began by telling me we are all the "apple of his eye" and he takes great care of what is his. He burns with a passion and love he has for all of us.

"Guard me as you would guard your own eyes.
Hide me in the shadow of your wings" (Ps. 17:8).

I am legally blind in my left eye. If you were to look at me it's barely detectible. It's considered a "lazy eye" and droops slightly if I'm extremely tired. Other than that, it appears normal. I requested Lasik surgery and the doctor shared an analogy of how my eye operates the same as a thirty-five-millimeter camera. (This was before the days of digital photography.)

"Your eye is a camera out of focus and not only is it out of focus you realize there is no film in the camera. There is nothing behind the pupil to alter," the doctor said.

If I were to rely on my left eye, within moments, a small "window" is visible in the middle, surrounded by black. There is no clarity in vision. The "window" gets darker and began to close the longer the right eye is covered. Knowing the risk of Lasik surgery, I was told the right eye was inoperable and the risk was too great to losing both eyes, rendering me legally blind.

I take great care of my eye, and as soon as something abnormal surfaces I go immediately to the ophthalmologist. When I read the verse I am the "apple of God's eye" for the first time as a child, immediately my heart sprang with joy how special I was to God.

Given my lack of vision, this verse has come to mean even more to me. The Bible says God guards and protects me the way I guard my right eye.

Thankfully, God's eye is never blurred, never blinded, never strained. God's love "always protects, always trusts, always hopes, always perseveres" (1 Cor. 13:7, NIV).

As an adult, I pondered these verses and realized that I didn't't know what this metaphor meant from a Biblical perspective. God has an apple in his eye? I'm the apple? I don't often dig into the original Hebrew version of scripture, but in this instance, I decided to do a little digging. As I searched what it meant I came across a website where another person was asking the same question.

What I found astonished me and once again, God was communicating through a simple verse. It is an Old Testament biblical phrase and consists of two Hebrew words.

The Hebrew word for apple is *ishon* and it refers to the pupil of the eye. The Hebrew word for eye is *ayin*. Apple of the eye: "Delicate part of the eye that is essential for vision and therefore must be protected at all costs … Apple of the eye is a reference to the part of the eye that reflects what one is looking at in life" (Adema, 2000). I am the center of God's vision.

In Deuteronomy 32:10, we find Moses speaking of how the Lord cared for Jacob. Verse 10 states, "In a desert land he found him, in a barren and howling waste. He shielded him and cared for him; he guarded him as the apple of his eye."

In Zechariah 2:8–9, we read, "For whoever touches you touches the apple of his eye." Proverbs 7:2 states, "Keep my commands and you will live; guard my teachings as the apple of your eye."

God reminded me in the book of Genesis and the fall of man; the Bible does not specify the fruit when Adam and Eve were in the Garden of Eden. I don't know when and why apple became the fruit that signifies when sin entered the world. It states only fruit (Gen. 3). People represent the apple as sin, however, where apple is specified in the Word, we are told we are special, resulting in something good, precious.

Matthew Henry was a Presbyterian pastor in the late 1600s. He did a commentary on Revelations 1, where John wrote "eyes pouring fire-blaze, both feet furnace-fired bronze …" He stated, "His eyes as a flame of fire, may represent his knowledge of the secrets of all hearts" (1706). I love when God validates what he grants from his presence through the Word and other godly resources.

I was overwhelmed with God's awesome power and loving embrace of spiritual sight that morning. What I didn't realize was in this moment, feeling the burning heart and love from God, was the beginning of his promise of protection for my children. It would come later in an image.

I began a new prayer strategy to intercede for the well-being of my boys. I began thanking God for how my children are not only the apple of my eye, but his. Over the course of a year, God worked miraculously and with exquisite detail in our family's life.

I love the thought that my children are at the center of God's eye. Thankfully, he sees all and meets our needs with amazing clarity and power. I had no idea how much God would give us, so we could continue boasting in the One who sees, loves, and redeems all.

Acknowledging God through worship, first and foremost, was the way I saw God's direction for my children, which wasn't vague or uncertain. The following chapters reveal how God directed our steps not just figuratively but literally. I continued to pay attention to the sequence of events he spoke into my spirit.

God's eyes burn like fire for all, and he cares no less for my children as he does for those suffering as Christ suffered. I wanted my children to find their own way walking with Christ, and my prayers were always that they would have their own experience and a "burning desire" for more of God.

In the subsequent pages, I will explain how God led our family and performed numerous miracles. The Israelites experienced and saw with their own eyes miracle after miracle. God's Word shows us he does not abandon us because that would dishonor his name (1 Sam. 12:22, NLT). The following pages contain some of our miracles; God's hand continually at work for the well-being of the Odden family.

A cornerstone of my prayers for my children is that they will have a burning desire for more of God, and their own testimonies to share of God's faithfulness. My prayers were answered.

"I don't wanna ride on somebody else's passion
I don't wanna find that I am just dry bones
I wanna burn with unquenchable fire deep
down inside see it coming alive
help me find my own flame, help me find my own fire,
I want the real thing, I want your burning desire
In my heart tonight do what only You can do"
(Will Reagan & United Pursuit, 2013).

Part 5

God-Dreams

7

Dreams of Hope or Fear?

"Since we see dreams with the eyes of the heart, we should not switch off the light in our hearts" (J. Ibojie).

Miracles in the Details

In the New Testament, there are several instances where verses from the Old Testament are reiterated. When scripture is repeated it catches my attention to take a closer look.

One of those messages in both the Old and New Testaments pertain to dreams and visions. "In the last days, God says, 'I will pour out my Spirit upon all people. Your sons and daughters will prophesy. Your young men will see visions, and your old men will dream dreams'" (Joel 2:28 and repeated in Acts 2:17, NLT).

God's promise, repeated, is "he will pour out his Spirit on all people," and I want to be included with the *all*. *Upon* means to be "on, to be attached, contact with something or someone" (Dictionary. com, 2015). I desire the Holy Spirit to be "on" me, to teach, and equip me for his overall purpose.

My *Parachute Dream* beautifully portrays when I am walking with God, he sweeps me away, clothing me in his righteousness, covered, protected.

I pray the same for my children. That God will cover and protect them. Unbeknownst to me, God was answering my prayers in ways I was unaware.

My friend Susan had a dream she knew was from the Lord and thankfully she took it seriously. It pertained to my son, Jacob. She shared her dream, asking me to pray for meaning and insight. She could have easily dismissed the dream because she lived in Michigan and Jacob in Minnesota. Susan had no communication with Jacob and didn't know what season of life he was in. What she didn't know, God did, and God spoke through her.

> *"Beauty overwhelms us, enchants us, fascinates us, and calls us" (Fr. Andrew Greeley).*

In my first book, *Beautiful Dreamer*, I shared the beauty of my God-given dreams and provided information about how we can seek God for insight and understanding. Overall, dreams are like riddles and the primary way for understanding is through prayer.

There is danger to misinterpretation if we ignore the importance of prayer. Without God's direction, I run the risk of walking my own way, which may be counterproductive to God's overall best for me. Of course I wanted God's best for Jacob.

I had no doubt the Lord would reveal and protect this message he had given through Susan for the proper time. My responsibility was to pray for insight and not neglect doing so.

At the time of Susan's dream, Jacob was not yet dating his wife, Emma. Susan was unaware if Jacob was dating. For several months the Holy Spirit provided bits of insight on different days, enough so that approximately five months later, I felt it was time to share the dream with Jacob and Emma (who were at that time engaged). I did not tell Susan I was forwarding the dream to them.

It wasn't until Jacob and Emma received the dream, and my initial interpretation, that the majority of the key message was revealed. There was a quickening in Emma's spirit because she had already been cultivating an atmosphere of prayer for their future. God's timing was perfect as always.

> *"Often, the language of the heart makes no sense to the*
> *mind except for those whose hearts are involved, because*
> *the heart lives in the language of love" (Goll, 2006).*

God was working supernaturally and through others. It is another beautiful way we can delight in how God knows all our needs and is always at work in our lives. I call this dream, *Dream across State Lines.*

Dream across State Lines
Susan Kahn

I (Susan) and my daughter, Erin, were with Jacob Odden. We met him at a café, located in a small town, enjoying coffee. Erin was about seven years old. I knew that Jacob would be living with a family in the inner city. There was an African American family in the dream. The three of us were sitting outside on the patio overlooking a beautiful lake. We hugged and greeted one another and when Jacob's mom, Teresa, approached us, she asked me about using the slang "love ya." She crinkled her nose and shook her head no and said "Susan, you shouldn't say that."

The four of us sat down, and I (Susan) felt in the dream I was supposed to come back and take Jacob shopping because Rick and Teresa were in Germany at the time of this dream. I looked at my calendar and told him I could come back at Thanksgiving.

Erin and Jacob took off down to the lake where beautiful boats were docked. Teresa and I walked behind but couldn't see them. Erin came running back with a small fishing pole, and I asked if Jacob had given it to her to keep or to borrow. Erin said Jacob gave it to her. Then I asked Erin to show us where Jacob was living. It was the first house at the end of the dock. There was a row of homes and his house number was 709.

We went in but didn't turn on the lights. From the light shining in through the window, we could see the house was very well kept. The walls were painted a cream color with blue trim. We walked into the kitchen, and there was a large opening into the dining room. We noticed on top of the refrigerator a beautiful spray of fresh flowers.
End of dream

God had already prepared Jacob and Emma's spirits with a readiness to understand and take action. God initiated a path, which became visible through the dream of another, for their passage as man and wife. What was unseen became known and what was made clear was a literal course of action.

"The man who is the most fully taught of God is the very one who will be most ready to listen to what God has" (Torrey, 1910).

Interpretation of Dream across State Lines

Jacob and Emma did not take this dream and fit it into their lives. They allowed God to speak to their spirit the purpose and guidance they had been praying for. What they were feeling in their spirits was confirmed from this dream.

The entire dream had a story and the story played out from past, present, and future. First, a promise there would be a spiritual increase for ministry, represented by the lake (boats docked, fishers of men). Susan was symbolic for God and his presence and friendship.

For many, coffee is the way we begin a new day. It stimulates our minds and gives us the boost we need to enter the day with energy and vitality. For Emma, the coffee represented a new day, a fresh start when she gave her heart to the Lord.

After Emma surrendered her life to God, she began working with youth. Jacob and Emma had been praying for a church they could begin ministry as a couple. When she worked with the youth, she was at Fountain of Life church. They felt in their hearts God was using the water in the dream to confirm this was the church they were to begin attending.

The docked boats also represented a time of waiting. In time, the boats would leave the dock and set sail, and in time, they would begin ministry (fishers of men). In the dream, Susan took Jacob shopping. It's an illustration how God takes care of us and meets all our needs. Once again, a simple way God was protecting and covering my child with his presence.

The first thing Jacob noticed about the dream was the house number 709. Sometimes the answers come through in the simplest ways. When hearing the dream, he opened his Bible, and there on page 709 was our family verse: "The Lord says, 'I will guide you along the best pathway for your life. I will advise you and watch over you'" (Ps. 32:8, NLT).

This was a beautiful and simple confirmation God was pointing the way and this was divine intervention. This aspect of the dream was so specific to their lives; it was cause to pay attention to and not look at it as if happenstance.

Unbeknownst to me, this was the beginning of how God would use numbers to validate his direction in the lives of my children. This was the starting point in the coming months to pay attention to numbers.

The beautiful thing about dreams is when left to God to interpret, he leaves little room for doubt. There is the human side that can cause error, but when things are from God, he will make all things clear. From the moment that Emma read the dream, it resonated with her in so many ways. She could clearly see how this dream represented where she had been and where God was leading her.

When Emma worked with the youth in the parsonage after her conversion, it was the same colors in the dream, blue and cream. She began to see how literally the dream aligned to her life with details Susan, Jacob, nor I were aware of. While living there she tore a wall down between the dining room and kitchen, creating a wide, open feel to the room for more light to come in. Emma always kept fresh flowers on top of the refrigerator. God revealed amazing details that aligned with Emma's former life and gave excitement of what to look forward to when they were married.

Additional notes from Jim Goll's book on symbol interpretation pertaining to key messages in this dream include: Water often represents Holy Spirit, ministry, church. It was a time of thanks (Thanksgiving), and the boats represent support, life, person, recreation, spare time. They were docked and ready.

Home in dreams can often represent family, security, church. In the dream they didn't turn the light on because in reality God is light. Not only is Jesus the light, but they were willing to let their light shine for Jesus by inviting others into their home.

Blue is symbolic for heavenly. Kitchen and table represented "come eat at the king's table," and a place of gathering, fellowship, sharing, breaking of bread. Large opening also allows more room for more people. Everything was very clean (heart, motive, stored in her heart, pure, white as snow) and spiritual restoration.

God had given exquisite detail of his direct involvement in their lives. We had much to boast of in God's love for my children and how he supernaturally and miraculously gave confirmation and direction. This dream was a certainty they were hearing what God wanted them to do, and he was already preparing the way for them.

> *"… God's praying servants had not the least doubt that prayer would work marvelous results and bring the supernatural into the affairs of earth. The miracle was the proof that God heard and answered prayer. The miracle was the divine demonstration that God, who was in heaven, interfered in earth's affairs, intervened to help men, and worked supernaturally if need be to accomplish his purposes in answer to prayer"* (Bounds, n.d., Chapter 13).

I now have a greater love and appreciation of how Jesus posed questions and illustrations that often perplexed his hearers. When Christ would share a parable, so often those listening didn't always understand and Jesus would follow-up, explaining the parable in words common to man. Those who were able to hear Jesus's message directly sat and listened with great anticipation. God did not send them on their way telling them to "figure it out."

That's how I felt when I first read Susan's dream for Jacob. We had no initial understanding to the meaning and importance of the dream. The dream was for Jacob and Emma to seek the Lord for insight and revelation. God answered.

I remain in the dark only when I remove God as the author of the message and when I'm a prayerless believer. God has shown me that the way to figure "it" out comes through his voice (prayer and absorbing the Bible).

Had Jacob and Emma ignored the personal and intimate relationship afforded to them by God Almighty, they may have missed God's perfect plans as they began their life as husband and wife.

A year and a half after this dream, they were married and moved into their first apartment. At the end of their first year of marriage, circumstances changed, and they had to move. It wasn't until I was proofing this section of the book that I recognized a deeper revelation had come to pass from this one dream. Dreams are one of those manifestations from God where revelation comes in stages. This was the case for Jacob and Emma.

"To every man there comes … that special moment when he is figuratively tapped on the shoulder and offered the chance to do a special thing unique to him and fitted to his talent. What a tragedy if that moment finds him unprepared or unqualified for the work which would be his finest hour" (Sir W. Churchill, n.d.).

Jacob was continuing his education and because of their low income, they qualified for a beautiful apartment with covered parking, which is a huge blessing in Minnesota winters. Ten months after their wedding, they received word they were now making too much to qualify for the lower apartment rent. Rent would go up $500 a month, an amount they could not afford with Jacob still in college.

They began looking for a new place to live. Through a friend, they were told of a house with three individuals living on the second floor and the first floor was available to rent. The complex had two staircases, one in front and one in the back of the house. Though they had privacy and their own living space, it also created access for community living and an environment to share time and meals together.

One of Emma's first comments to me was how this change would open doors for them to live in community and what it means to be part of others' lives on a daily basis. To live in "community," she said, was the season God had for them (boats in the docks and now taking off and fishers of men, interpretation from the dream).

Sitting down in the cafe, taking the fishing pole, clearly outlined how Jacob and Emma immediately began cooking and preparing meals for the group and opening their home and hearts to others. Experiences and words from the Lord shouldn't surprise us, but time and time again, God astonishes me by how he guides specifically.

It wasn't until this time I also recognized their church was in the inner-city and low income section of town. Statistically, low-income neighborhoods are primarily inhabited by minorities due to the institutional and structural racism that still exists in the United States. The African American family in the dream confirmed this was the area God wanted them to live. During their first year of marriage, I had great comfort because I saw them living in God's will.

I've read it's often not necessary to pick apart every detail of dreams and to focus primarily on key components. However, my personality looks for details from God, and when I hear a dream and pray about it, I get excited thinking about how involved my God wants to be in my life.

When we thought all was revealed, God used this dream to once again show them how he is involved in the detail of their lives. It wouldn't be for some time that we understood Emma entering the home alone also represented her bringing the light of Jesus into her home and marriage. Jacob had not yet entered into this level of spiritual maturity, thus, still playing around, having fun. Greater understanding was revealed where Jacob was between the boats represented by Erin in the dream, waiting for ministry, and meeting up with Emma, to be walking together in ministry and maturity in Christ.

God provided insight how to pray strategically for Jacob and Emma. I didn't know that Jacob had not yet stepped into his role as a husband and was still behaving childishly (represented by Erin). They went through some trying times, including two miscarriages.

I love Susan's dream because it reveals God's personal touch on our lives and the joy that comes when we pray for someone and God gives specific direction on how to pray. It reveals the power of our prayers when God brings to mind a loved one to pray for. We may not see what's going on, but God is always at work.

Because of Susan's faithfulness to hear God and step out in faith to share this dream, Jacob and Emma now have a God-story of their own to tell. It is a beautiful start of life together as man and wife, with words of wisdom and faithfulness. It is also a lesson for me to never underestimate what God wants to do when I know he has spoken clearly. My responsibility for my son and his wife was and remains simply to pray.

As I continued along my spiritual journey, God continued to reveal the beauty of his sacrifice and cleansing from sin. I call it *Fatherly Love Dream*.

Fatherly Love Dream

I walked into a house, where there were two, very short men who I found immature. There was another gentleman who was very large and much older. The two men asked if I wanted a beer and handed me a drink. I took a sip and it tasted bitter. I wanted to spit it out. I couldn't believe they found this appealing.

I went outside with the larger, older gentleman, and he picked something up from the ground. He looked at it and I saw it was a worm. He shrugged it off as though it were no big deal. He asked me if I had the same thing and I didn't want to tell him I had a worm in my bicep. I could see the worm inside my arm as though I was looking at an x-ray. The worm was small, white, translucent. The gentleman said nothing, looked at my bicep, and extracted the worm.

As we stood outside, another man ran up to us, screaming. He had a severe rash with boils and red blotches all over his body. As he ran screaming he showed us his back. Continuing to scream and throwing his arms all over the place, he ran in panic in the house. We came back into the house and it was then I realized the larger, older man, was the father of the three men (two at the beginning who were immature and now the third one running in a panic because of his pain). When the sick man entered, the other two sons started yelling at each other. I stood there and said to the three sons how their father picked a worm from the ground and also removed the worm from my body.

End of dream

Interpretation of Fatherly Love Dream

> *"The cuts in my flesh stink and grow maggots because I've lived so badly"* (Ps. 38:5–8, MSG).

Because I grew up in an alcoholic home, God used a dream I could relate to. A "language" that comes from my life's experience, things that make sense to me that may mean nothing to someone else.

The two young men represented my childhood, my past. The taste of beer was bitter and I didn't want to be in the same room with the two young men. I also recognized that had I continued along my path of drinking I too would be an alcoholic.

The older man symbolized my heavenly Father and how easy he plucks and removes sin and residue from my life. Joe Ibojie's worm definition is "something that eats from the inside, often secretly. Not obvious on the surface. Disease, filthiness" (2005).

The third son with the rash came running, representing how sin may look. His sin was out in the open, whereas mine was lurking within. A reminder how easy it is to ignore those things nobody can see. The worm that remained in my arm was the *residue* of things I may not recognize.

I tried to hide the white, translucent worm in my arm, but he (representing Christ) saw what nobody else could see. I can rest peacefully and allow my heavenly Father to extract what remains; otherwise I run the risk of being infected by other sins that spread.

This dream resonated with me and in the way of my limited understanding how computer viruses, often defined as a "worm virus," can cause great harm and *infect* a system. Most often when the computer has a worm virus, it is not visible until it hits the network and affects many parts of the computer or multiple parts of a corporations network (Beal, 2014).

"A computer virus attaches itself to a program or file enabling it to spread from one computer to another, leaving infections as it travels. Like a human virus, a computer virus can range in severity: some may cause only mildly annoying effects while others can damage your hardware, software or files" (Beal, 2014).

The *Fatherly Love Dream* is a gripping illustration of the need for cleansing from sin, but a beautiful scene because God is love and always willing and able to forgive and cleanse fully. He does so gently and without condemnation.

The white, translucent worm is a beautiful picture of how God has cleansed my heart and made me "white as snow." I believe the greater meaning of the white, translucent worm is to accept God's forgiveness and let go of guilt and condemnation, unlike the son who rushed past, unwilling to accept the Father's help. How God redeems! With no effort of my own, other than to willingly accept his grace of forgiveness.

Many times in my life, I remember sins from my childhood, things I know I've been forgiven for, but there is this nagging guilt and condemnation. After all these years, there are moments when thoughts sink into my mind, causing a sense of condemnation and need for total freedom. I know these are attacks from the enemy, who continually tries to steal my joy that is found in Christ.

It wouldn't be for a few years after the *Fatherly Love Dream* God gave me another dream that brought total healing from past condemnation. I must be vigilant to see the enemy around me in order to receive God's best for my life. Only God can help me identify those things that trigger emotions festering within, which have not been fully dealt with.

"Even if I scrub myself all over and wash myself with the strongest soap I can find, It wouldn't last—you'd push me into a pigpen, or worse, so nobody could stand me for the stink" (Job 9:25–31).

Another verse that illustrates God operating in my life is found in Mark 1:40–42: "A leper came to him, begging on his knees, 'If you want to, you can cleanse me.' Deeply moved, Jesus put out his hand, touched him, and said, 'I want to. Be clean'" (MSG).

I love finding verses that adequately articulate what God has planted in my spirit. What a beautiful verse to bring to life my dream. A dream not only for spiritual healing, but for physical healing. Because the Word of God is familiar, I have a tendency to skim, even skip scripture. I have to remind myself that God's Word is the most important source of knowledge that exists to mankind.

Acknowledging this and believing that the power of the Word of God is living and life-changing, I want people to recognize the Word first and foremost before any other words written in this book.

My words and that of any other should be secondary to God's perfect and powerful Word. I can be confident God will validate his direction through scripture, but I must know it, study it.

Given the number of visions and dreams I'm sharing I wish to remind you, God brings revelation supernaturally. God is like no other. He is simply, yet powerfully supernatural in all he does. And everything he does is for his glory, which he exhibits by his unfailing love, grace, and faithfulness.

The next dream, I call *Black Pearls Dream*, and the dream is a story that led to total redemption, forgiveness, and God's protection. I didn't realize at the time the multiple ways in which God would use this dream to discern the presence of the enemy.

Satan had planted a subliminal message into my subconscious with the intention to take my eyes off God. God, however, used this dream to teach, guide, and encourage, though it was disguised with appearance for alarm.

I have no doubt that had I not been walking daily with a ready supply of God's Word and presence, this dream would have caused concern and unrest. However, being a praying believer, what appeared to be a disgusting and dreadful dream, God used to bring peace.

Once again, the order and details from previous dreams were significant. The family in the *Fatherly Love Dream* provided strategies of how to pray specifically for my children. I asked God to reveal whatever may be *lurking* within their hearts to hear him, and recognize what needs to be extracted for them to live a life pleasing to him.

It isn't an easy thing to ask God to bring what is in the dark and into the light. However, when there are things only God can see that need redeeming, he will extend the same grace to them as he has done so many times for me.

The majority of people seeking God through other religions believe in the invisible and evil forces in the world. All may not acknowledge the devil exists, but many acknowledge evil spirits.

I'm amazed how many episodes are on television about aliens, ghosts, and the paranormal. There is clear interest in the world for unseen forces and a desire to seek them out. I would rather speak more of God's spiritual presence, the presence and Spirit of Truth, than that of the devil and his army of deception and despair.

God's Word warns us that the devil prowls around looking for someone to devour (1 Pet. 5:8). The hope I have is God's promises will demolish unseen forces through Jesus Christ (2 Cor. 10:4). The Bible also tell us we are to flee temptation and stand firm against the devil (James 4:7). The devil and his army are real, but God's army is bigger. The cosmic battle has already been decided. It is only the battle for the soul of every man that remains. The Bible doesn't say to deny the devil, but it does say deny yourself.

Again, another reminder of the importance for God to empty me, so I can walk confidently with the Holy Spirit clothing and guiding me into all Truth.

I can stand confidently trusting the Holy Spirit to help me discern demonic forces. God is protector, deliverer, and provider and I need not fear. As I trust him, he will activate the Holy Spirit to step in for my well-being. God has won and offers his power to me, but I must pray for discernment to recognize the enemy. I knew God would do the same for my children.

> *"Let us discern for ourselves what is right; let us learn together what is good" (Job 34:4, NLT).*

Black Pearls Dream

There was a girl who received a gift of gray and black pearls. When she put them on, the necklace tightened and started choking her. She tried speaking and the harder she tried, the weaker she became. She couldn't catch her breath. Struggling, she tried to yank off the necklace. It wasn't until then I realized the girl was me. Though I couldn't see a face of the one who gave me the pearls, I exchanged words and our conversation was one where we were going back and forth, stirring up doubt and confusion. I struggled trying to break free from the necklace. There was someone standing in the back watching, doing nothing. I remember a friend from my childhood who recently moved. She was cuddling her granddaughter. I was bothered she wasn't coming to my rescue.
End of dream

When I woke up, fear was present, and I knew it was a dream the devil planted in my subconscious. The black pearls represented darkness, evil, but the pearls were a disguise because they are beautiful and an example of something precious. I was assaulted by the choking of the pearls and overwhelmed with a sense of defeat and a feeling that I had nowhere to go. But I knew and know there is always a way to go when we are with Christ. God will never "strangle" us to the point of death, for God is Love and Life.

The *Black Pearls Dream* is a great example and reminder of why I ask God to fill my spirit with peace while I sleep and ask him to speak to me through dreams and visions. Thankfully, where the devil tries to distract, God always reveals and diverts the plans of the enemy.

The pearls and the baby together in one dream represented beauty, innocence, and something sweet. Because of my unrest within the dream, I recognized what appeared innocent was a diversion to think it was a gift from the Lord. It goes back to how God "originates in the Holy Spirit and fire" and will give discernment to know light from darkness, good from evil.

> *"I sing to God, the Praise-Lofty, and find myself safe and saved. The hangman's noose was tight at my throat; devil waters rushed over me. Hell's ropes cinched me tight; death traps barred every exit" (Ps. 18:3–5 MSG).*

God continually reminds me, "Know the Word, I'm your teacher, ask for help." *If I don't know the Word, I don't know him, and when I don't know him, it limits my intake of his presence and the outcome of his power.* His presence is necessary to discern his voice.

The anxiety of uncertainty in the dream bred confusion. God is never confused nor does he cause confusion. The Voice of God may not convey the message you want to hear (such was the case with my *Campfire and Rocky Road Visions*), but he always brings peace. It is his promises in the Word: "For God is not the author of confusion, but of peace …" (1 Cor. 14:33, NKJV).

The dream reminded me to refrain from communicating with the enemy (which I believe the conversation in the dream symbolized). The more I tried to convince, the weaker I became, to the point my breath was cut off (strangling represented how the enemy wants to hold me back, God does not).

I think dwelling on that which is negative and with a pessimistic attitude can be one way that we find ourselves conversing with the enemy. God wants me to speak blessings and give voice to the good he is doing in my life. Not to focus on what I don't see and what is negative.

God is infinite and the multitude of answered prayers and the way he guided and guides are all miracles. I continued praying and pleading on behalf of my sons. As my prayers for my children continued, over and over, God stepped in with his great power, might, and love, loving on me, loving on my kids.

God provided insight, wisdom, and pictures through which I could see hope, not hopelessness. The older I get, the more I realize there are no substitutes for knowing God. When I look for short-cuts to knowing and hearing God, there is a greater chance I will operate on my own and frankly, it's too dangerous to make life-altering decisions apart from my God who is all-knowing. *I must spend time with God to know God and to know his will for my life.*

"God doesn't come and go. God lasts. he's Creator of all you can see or imagine. He doesn't get tired out, doesn't pause to catch his breath. And he knows everything, inside and out" (Isa. 40:27–31 MSG).

Part 6

Outrageous Miracles

8

A Son's Promise—A Mother's Persistence

"Your life is a journey you must travel with a deep consciousness of God. It cost God plenty to get you out of that dead-end, empty-headed life you grew up in. he paid with Christ's sacred blood, you know. He died like an unblemished, sacrificial lamb. And this was no afterthought. Even though it has only lately—at the end of the ages—become public knowledge, God always knew he was going to do this for you. It's because of this sacrificed Messiah, whom God then raised from the dead and glorified, that you trust God, that you know you have a future in God" (1 Pet. 1:18–21, MSG).

God planted in my spirit a very lengthy dream. I had no doubt upon waking up this was from God. What follows is a partial section of the dream. I extracted what is important to convey God's overall message about the beginning of my son Alex's journey and God's perfect will for him. I call it *College Campus Dream to Intercede.*

College Campus Dream to Intercede

My son (Alex) was with one of the friends he met during his first semester in college (literal friend). It was 3:00 a.m., and I looked out a campus window and saw them walking through the park. My thought in the dream was hopefulness that he wasn't getting caught up in university partying, which is so prevalent among college students.

The scene changed to winter, and the campus was full of life with students sledding to my left. I recognized what I was seeing was good, old fashion, clean fun. Kids were dressed in mascot colors, with their faces and bodies painted green and white, ready for game day. They were at my husband's alma mater (Michigan State University). I knew it would be like Alex to be in this crowd because he always dresses up in team colors. I was looking for him, but it was dark and I couldn't see him.

As the scene progressed, I was able to pick him out by his walk. He was leaving campus, but now with his long-time friend from childhood, Jordan.

End of dream

College Campus Dream Interpretation

I woke up with the impression I should "listen up." I had no doubt God was guiding how to pray for him. From this dream, I began praying specifically God would bring into light what might be hidden, (hidden sin as pictured in the *Fatherly Love Dream*) if anything. Walking represented progress and I prayed strategically Alex would develop and make spiritual progress.

Walking to the window represented the future. Alex would be set apart from where he currently was. Both friends were doing their own thing, away from the crowd. Snow—fresh, new, beautiful, pure.

I began praying God would prepare a fresh start for Alex and direct his steps.

A reminder from Proverbs 22:6 that Alex should go his way, not his parents' way. "Train up a child in the way he should go, and when he is old he will not depart from it" (NIV).

At the time of this dream, we weren't certain if Alex would leave traditional education to learn the trade of a commercial, deep-sea diver (which he had discussed with his father). Doing so would mean not only leaving traditional education, but also the city he had grown up in (represented by his friend Jordan).

When my son made his announcement to go into the commercial diving field, it was brought to our attention that the industry was rife with heavy alcohol and drug abuse. We were told by a few, "it is an environment of drugs and alcohol." Hearing discouraging and unkind words stirs up unrest and anxiety.

I prayed against a judgmental spirit in myself and others, knowing that our words result in blessings or curses. Did negative, judgmental words carry power, a prophetic curse on my son's life? I would like to think not, but I also know a critical spirit is powerful.

> *"Do not pick on people, jump on their failures, criticize their faults—unless, of course, you want the same treatment. That critical spirit has a way of boomeranging" (Matt. 7:1, MSG).*

Thankfully, we were encouraged by many family friends who were intrigued about Alex's prospect of a unique career with such a specific skill set. When negative "arrows" are directed toward my family, I often pray and ask God to turn them around and back to the one who threw them (Ps. 64).

The truth is, I know I've been guilty of the same, and need God's continual guidance to see people the way he does. It is a reminder to watch my own words. I don't want my "arrows" boomeranging. I want to fear God so my words and actions lead to grace for others the way God has granted the same love and grace to me, and in abundance.

> *"They sharpen their tongues like swords and aim their bitter words like arrows. They shoot from ambush at the innocent, attacking suddenly and fearlessly. "Who will ever notice?" they ask. Yes, the human heart and mind are cunning. But God himself will shoot them with his arrows, suddenly striking them down. Their own tongues will ruin them, and all who see them will shake their heads in scorn. Then everyone will be afraid; they will proclaim*

the mighty acts of God and realize all the amazing things he does.
The godly will rejoice in the Lord and find shelter in him. And
those who do what is right will praise him" (Ps. 64, NLT).

While my son was enjoying his extended Christmas holiday with us in Germany, I had two dreams I failed to write down. I remembered but a few details and later learned they were sufficient for the path God was directing. Over the course of a year God worked miraculously in an assortment of ways. I do not use *miraculously* lightly.

Doug Addison states that often the dreams we can't remember are the best dreams "because God has divinely sealed our instructions. I call it, 'revelation with no obligation'" (Addison, 2013). I've found this to be true.

It doesn't matter how many times God speaks or the manner in which he speaks, he continually refreshes my soul. I cannot afford to live without the nourishment of God's presence and direction.

I have no doubt Jesus took my prayers for Alex and embellished them to the Father, ensuring my limited understanding of needs were articulated in ways I did not know. God is Truth and there will never be misinterpretation of my requests before God that aren't for my well-being and that of my children. "The Lord directs the steps of the godly. He delights in every detail of their lives" (Ps. 37:23, NLT).

God's plans for our life does not have to be abstract. In fact, I don't find in scripture that I have to keep guessing. It's quite the opposite. God tells us to press on with endurance by asking for wisdom and expecting an answer. James 1 states if we have particular problems we should ask God and we can be certain he will not only grant us wisdom, but he says he will give it in abundance. The New International Version uses the word *generously*. If we believe, we ask. If we ask, we know God gives generously, therefore, guessing to me is unbelief.

I can't even begin to count how many people continue to ask me how they can hear God. Two words: Bible and prayer. There is this resistance to doing what is so simple to knowing and hearing God.

So when people ask me, "how do know God's plans for your life?" the prerequisite is to read the Bible and pray. When we read the Bible, we are given the instructions straight from the Living God, the Living Word. We will hear God when we read the Bible and it tunes our ears to hear him speak into our spirits when we pray. When he speaks, there is absolutely no doubt; you will know it is him.

James 1 is just one promise in the Bible that we are told we can know with certainty what God wants us to do. "The man who trusts God, but with inward reservations, is like a wave of the sea, carried forward by the wind one moment and driven back the next. That sort of man cannot hope to receive anything from God, and the life of a man of divided loyalty will reveal instability at every turn" (James 1:2–8, Phillips).

Guessing would keep me in a state of confusion without enough information what to do or where to go. The Bible says God is not the author of confusion; therefore, we don't have to wander and wonder what he is saying (1 Cor. 14:33). This means he will always give us something, though it might be small, it is always sufficient for what we need at the time. It may come simply through a verse to hold on while we wait for further instructions.

God does not leave us hanging in the balance if we look for direction, but it may take time in his presence to hear him with certainty. A delayed response of any kind isn't God's doing, it's mine. I have to be accountable for not hearing God's will for my life and I wonder how many times I was just seconds away from getting an answer from God, but I got up and went about my business of the day.

His promises guide us to ask, wait, and expect. When I believe in the Word of God, I can wait with patience and confidence knowing that I'm right where I need to be until he moves me a step further. Prayer, reading of the Word of God is how and where you will discover God's will for your life. His voice is distinct from any other.

I'm continually amazed how explicit God is when I need clarity. A conscious effort of trusting and allowing God to be actively involved in our affairs results in hope, peace, and a positive outlook for the present and future.

When Alex graduated from the commercial diving academy we continued to pray God would open doors for employment. As a result, God provided supernatural deliverance with point-by-point instructions. May these accounts bring glory to God, who says, "Let the one who boasts, boast in the Lord" (2 Cor. 10:17, NIV). "Since many are boasting in the way the world does, I too will boast" (2 Cor. 11:18, NIV). To conceal these miracles would be to hide God's glory.

"He will be gracious to you if you ask for help ... he will still be with you. You will see your teacher with your own eyes, and you will hear a voice say, 'This is the way, turn around and walk here" (Isa. 30:19–21, NLT).

Lockers and Keys Dream

There was a locker room with three lockers connected. The two on the left had doors, and the one on the right had no door. In the middle of the open locker was an extremely large, round key-ring. The ring had numerous keys, which filled the entire ring.
End of dream

Partial Interpretation of Lockers and Keys Dream

"God, open doors for Alex as a commercial diver. Create a job that doesn't exist and ready it to be filled" (represented by the open locker), I prayed. I asked God to open many doors of opportunity (multiple keys) and expand his skills.

I went so far to ask God that an existing employee would leave and Alex would arrive at the right time to be hired as a replacement, regardless of his lack of experience. "God provide for my son," I prayed daily.

I believe God's children get preferential treatment, and I trusted God would go before him and give favor. I prayed with boldness, meaning I didn't hold back voicing my concerns, frustrations, and requests. "And how bold and free we then become in his presence, freely asking according to his will, sure that he's listening. And if we're confident that he's listening, we know that what we've asked for is as good as ours" (1 John 5:14–15, MSG).

The ultimate journey had just begun.

God's Precision

> *"From the very first day, we were there, taking it all in—we heard it with our own ears, saw it with our own eyes, verified it with our own hands. The Word of Life appeared right before our eyes; we saw it happen! And now we're telling you in most sober prose that what we witnessed was, incredibly, this: The infinite Life of God himself took shape before us. We saw it, we heard it, and now we're telling you so you can experience it along with us, this experience of communion with the Father and his Son, Jesus Christ. Our motive for writing is simply this: We want you to enjoy this, too. Your joy will double our joy! (1 John 1:1–4, MSG).*

To reach someone via telephone you have to dial in the specific number. If you misdial by one number, you will not reach the intended party. The numbers must be precise and numbers with God work the same way. They are absolute. In the same way God used the number 709 for Jacob and Emma, God gave two specific numbers and later a third in dreams related to Alex and his journey.

Alex didn't know the direction he was going, but the morning he set off in search of a job, in a new city, God "created a pathway no one knew was there" (Ps. 77:19 and 80:9, NLT). Alex didn't know which direction to go and started each morning in prayer. Through prayer there was a confidence God would lead the way as promised in Psalm 77. There is no doubt God began supernaturally fashioning together miracles to boast in.

Number 84 and 3467 Dreams

I had two dreams with numbers. The first I remembered only num-ber 84 and the word pregnancy. *In the second dream I was trying to open a door, punching into a key pad the number 3467.*
End of dreams

God extends extravagant grace and he never ceases to amaze me by his goodness and guidance with complete accuracy. I had an incredible sense of God's provision and peace from these two dreams.

I always look to God for specific details, and sometimes I get them; sometimes I don't. Either way, I had no doubt God was oper-ating "behind the scenes," and I continually anticipated clear direc-tions. God came through every time on our behalf. Once again, God's plans don't have to be vague because there is nothing found in scripture that tells us we won't hear his voice clearly.

I began each day thanking God for guiding me this far and praised him for giving beautiful pictures during a time of uncertainty. I stood firm knowing God's best was present. By doing so, my mind filled with the word "pregnancy" from the dream, which represented birth, a new beginning.

I continued asking God to reveal the meanings of 84 and 3467, while continuing to intercede strategically from the *College Campus Dream*. I asked God to give Alex a heart to turn from sin, pray, listen, and hear his voice.

When Alex returned to the States, his primary goal was to obtain one final certification. He had no job and no place to live. He stayed a few weeks with family in Georgia. Once he obtained that last certification his plans were to drive to Houston, Texas. A fellow student from commercial diving was living there and found employ-ment so it seemed the logical place to start.

I journaled that I felt New Orleans was the place for him, but he was confident work was in Houston. I had this "nagging" feeling, which is most often the prompting by the Holy Spirit, to pray Alex would change direction.

I asked Alex if he prayed about going to Houston, and he said he did. I had no reason to think otherwise. If he wasn't praying, I was! I trusted God and prayed only what he impressed upon my heart.

Alex was on his own, with no money, and prepared to live out of his car if living arrangements fell through. God can do anything, so I prayed for what only God could do. "Lord, orchestrate a free place to stay and a job in the commercial diving field. Provide the finances to get him by until he secures employment," I prayed.

GOD CAN DO ANYTHING SO I PRAYED
FOR WHAT ONLY HE CAN DO.

Nevertheless, there continued to be unrest in my spirit. Unrest meaning an anxiousness because I had no control over the outcome as to where he would live and work. Daily, I had to fight the enemy by faithfully professing with my mouth the details of God's promises through these dreams.

I looked over these dreams regularly, and they were a constant strength to hold on to what I did not see. I was learning a new level of trust in God when it came to my children. I didn't want the enemy "choking" my joy away for what God had prepared for my son.

The framework for praying for Alex came from the brief details of these two dreams and every verse God was impressing upon my heart. I continually called upon God to reveal what 84 and 3467 meant.

It was during this time of waiting God began showing me that I insult him by not making my request known to him. My lack of trust to "ask anything in his name" results in slighting God as Creator of all things. Otherwise, I walk with a lack of expectation for his intervention. It was a beautiful period in my life where God continued to affirm "come with me, be with me, trust me."

"God is the Father of light—and if you fill your heart with God, then light will shine in … Therefore, we should prepare the spiritual soil of our heart for whatever dreams God may give us" (Ibojie, 2005).

God's Highway

Miracles of 84 and 3467 Number Dreams

"Let them see that this is your doing, that You yourself have done it, Lord" (Ps. 109:27, NLT).

The verse in Psalm 109 became a daily prayer of mine. Verses are promises, not just words to make me feel good, though it does that too. I wanted the world to see it was by God's hand and no other that all my son's needs were taken care of. I wanted people to recognize the possibilities that take place when we have confidence in God alone. I wanted people to believe in their own miracles and how God's love extends to those who relinquish control and allow him to orchestrate events in our lives. It was the beginning of seeing how divine intervention is most often initiated by prayer.

Alex called to let us know he left Georgia and instead of heading to Houston he told us he was heading to Louisiana. As a mother, I rejoiced because the Lord continued to whisper how to pray he would head toward New Orleans. Though small, I recognized this was one answer to my prayers. It was God's doing, not mine.

Surprised, but pleased, I asked why the change from Texas to Louisiana. He was given a place to stay. "Thank you God for your provisions, for another answer to prayer!"

While driving, Alex grabbed the sheet of paper with the address on it. He read the address that he had jotted down and gave me the address in Shriever, Louisiana. Having never heard of this city, I hung up and typed the address into Google Maps. I wanted to see how long his drive would be.

When I pressed *enter* after plugging in the address, I looked at the directions and the first point was routing him on *Highway 84*—the exact number from my first dream. I finally had an understanding why God put this number in my spirit and it gave me confidence my son was heading in the right direction. *Miracle from the first number.*

It would have been easy to dismiss a dream remembering only a number. God kept it simple, and it was what we needed. Interestingly, Highway 84 was first built starting in Georgia and was extended through Louisiana. This was again, a bit of information that encouraged me to keep trusting. God is a God of exquisite detail.

The joy I felt that morning was indescribable. I shouldn't be surprised how God steps in supernaturally, because he does so time and time again, with the caveat—if I'm listening, looking, and obeying. Looking not just during the day, but also in the night. Seeing Highway 84 was Alex's first route and without doubt, driving the King's Highway!

Though I call Highway 84 miracle number one, I believe all answered prayers are miracles. Seeing how God brings to fruition his divine plan in our lives was where I began to redefine a *miracle*. A miracle being an extraordinary answer to prayer stemming from something I cannot do for myself (Miracle, Dictionary.com). A need for divine intervention and God's hand to do what surpasses human reasoning. Something I cannot do on my own. God has said to me, *"If you don't put yourself in a position to receive a miracle, you won't experience miracles."*

God was stretching me to wait with expectation that divine intervention was near. I trusted God with my son's lives when we moved to Germany, and I had to continue believing God was preparing yet another miracle.

DIVINE INTERVENTION IS MOST
OFTEN INITIATED BY PRAYER.

The story of Gideon stood out. Gideon talked candidly with God after receiving God's instruction how to fight the battle. The result was God's intervention in the battle, which was won through prayer and simply talking with God (Judg. 6 and 7).

Another instance is the story of Sodom and Gomorrah. God spoke to Abraham that he was going to destroy the city due to the moral decay, evil, and wickedness in the town. Abraham interceded for the people asking God if he found fifty innocent people would he save the city. God said *yes*, but Abraham continued to negotiate. Abraham went a step further and said "Since I have begun, let me go and speak further to my Lord ... Suppose there are forty-five ... suppose forty ... suppose thirty ...?" God continued to say *yes*.

God kept saying *yes*, but Abraham didn't stop asking. "Since I have dared to speak to the Lord, let me continue—suppose there are only twenty ..." If that weren't enough, once again, Abraham continued, "Finally, Abraham said, 'Lord, please do not get angry; I will speak but once more,'" asking if only ten were innocent would he save the entire city. Unfortunately, God already knew there weren't ten innocent people, but because God loves us so much, he let Abraham speak to him honestly and to intercede for those in Sodom and Gomorrah (Gen. 18, NLT).

The lesson for me is to never stop asking God. I may not get what I want, but God is so loving to let me process my heart, my thoughts, including my pain and sorrow. This was a tragic event in history, but it reveals God's love for us, even in the midst where justice was required.

Little time and especially no time with God often increases the risk of overlooking what God is doing. Another reason why someone may continue to question yet another reason: "How do I know God's will for my life?" This is what happened with Saul in the Old

Testament. To pay little attention reduces the ability to recognize and acknowledge God. When we don't recognize who God is, it's no wonder people don't know what God is saying.

UNPLANNED TIME HAS OFTEN LEFT NO TIME WITH GOD. NO TIME WITH GOD CLOSES MY EARS TO HEAR.

Miracle Two—Number 3467

"The very steps we take come from God; otherwise how would we know where we're going" (Prov. 20:24, MSG).

After I searched the directions, I wanted to know more about the city. What was the population, how far was it from New Orleans (the only city I'd been to in Louisiana)? I was looking for anything to get a feel for where my son was going to live.

When I looked up Shriever, which included the P.O. Box number, my eyes immediately drifted to city addresses. I looked at zip codes and staring at me from my computer screen were the last four digits of his address, which was *3467*. Exactly the number in my dream.

God totally *wowed* me, again. Another miracle along his journey, but not the last. Initially they appeared insignificant, but as God has shown me, nothing in our lives is insignificant when God is behind it.

Had these been the only two verifiable miracles along his journey, I have no doubt it would have been sufficient to stay the course. I had miracles to hold onto and God provide me with assurance to see firsthand how he was leading. Because God is full of love and generosity, he didn't limit his detailed confirmations—something we would come to see later as divine intervention. God was doing something extraordinary.

The beauty of God's perfection is irrefutable and it shows how he is not limited by circumstances or time. He sealed those numbers in heaven and at the appropriate time, brought heaven to earth. "... Thy will be done, on earth as it is in heaven" (Matt. 6:10, KJV).

I proceeded to record Alex's journey, so when it was all said and done, God's great power would be glorified. Again, everyone would see it was his doing. "Praise the Lord and his marvelous works and wonders. Praise his Holy Name. Thank you Lord for allowing me to pray continually for my son. I know you have work for him. He wants to get offshore immediately, and I ask you to give him the desires of his heart. I'm so excited for him. Lord, I praise you!" I journaled.

Through these God-dreams, he once again, nourished my soul and gave me the fuel to see Alex's journey to the end, but the end leading to a new beginning.

"The God who made the world and everything in it, this Master of sky and land, doesn't live in custom-made shrines or need the human race to run errands for him, as if he couldn't take care of himself. He makes the creatures; the creatures don't make him. Starting from scratch, he made the entire human race and made the earth hospitable, with plenty of time and space for living so we could seek after God, and not just grope around in the dark but actually find him. He doesn't play hide-and-seek with us. He's not remote; he's near. We live and move in him, can't get away from him!" (Acts 17:27–29, MSG).

Resume the Journey—Unnoticeable Provisions

"... There is power far greater on our side! ... He may have a great army, but they are just men. We have the Lord our God to help us and to fight our battles for us!" (2 Chron. 32:7–8, NLT).

Pregnancy Gives Birth

The concept of "pregnancy" from the dream was still unclear, with no insight of how this word connected to the numbers. It seemed isolated and perhaps it meant nothing at all. Often, details in dreams can be dismissed. However, if there is purpose from them, God would give insight at the proper time. I continued to ask God to bring "new life" into Alex's circumstances.

God was slowly putting the pieces together, but we didn't know what pieces were needed to complete the picture. As our journey continued, for my faith not to waiver, it was imperative I remain in prayer. If I didn't put my heart and soul in a place of worship, prayer, and reading the Word, my peace was significantly reduced. Deficiency of prayer meant no peace. No peace resulted in fear and doubt.

These two numbers were reminders to not give up, but they also filled my spirit to keep looking with anticipation for greater things from God. What I also recognized is no matter how great the miracle, *I could not rely solely on yesterday's miracles. I had to keep my eyes open and believe God desires to do more.*

*A DEFICIENCY OF PRAYER MEANT NO PEACE.
NO PEACE RESULTED IN FEAR AND DOUBT.*

I love how Bill Johnson phrases past miracles, "It is up to us to keep the impact of an old experiment current" (p. 75). God always has something up his sleeve.

I continued to believe, pray, and journal. I recorded in my journal: "The Lord will open the doors for employment. I know it, believe it, and thank God for his provisions in Alex's life and meeting all his needs. He is alone, without family, job, or money. My God is bigger than any company or corporation. God can and will create a position for him. I praise the Lord for the miracles taking place. Believe, simply believe."

Nevertheless, many days I had unrest in my spirit. The enemy would attack my mind with anxiety that my child was alone. I found myself wanting to see where Alex was going. God would gently remind me to not allow doubt and unbelief to *choke* and steal my joy from what I didn't see. "Rest in me," God would gently reiterate. I needed rest and peace not only spiritually, but physically and mentally.

As the days continued, there was no visible sign that Alex's needs were being met. I continued to praise and worship the Lord. God lead me to 2 Chronicles 20 (NLT) and the account of the army Jehoshaphat was up against. He didn't know what to do; therefore, he "sought the Lord for guidance" (v. 3). God showed me I was doing exactly what he wanted me to do; seeking him.

In answer to Jehoshaphat's prayers, God spoke through another man, Jahaziel, to not be afraid or discouraged for the battle was not theirs, but the Lord's (v. 15). Through this man, God gave instructions—very strange instructions on how to fight and defeat the aggressing army. God told them not to fight but to "stand still and watch the Lord's victory" (v. 17).

Instead, they were to worship and praise the Lord. Once again, God was telling me, "Do not stop worshipping me, regardless of what you see and don't see."

Just as God said, Jehoshaphat appointed singers to go ahead of his army and lead them by singing to the Lord and praising him for his Holy Splendor. They were obedient and did what seemed illogical to win a war (verse 21).

God blessed their obedience and delivered them. The enemies started fighting amongst themselves! The people of God never lifted a finger to fight the battle. The Lord did all of it (vv. 22–26). In their obedience to do what seemed quite odd, "the Lord had rewarded them greatly. And from it, "… the kingdom of Jehoshaphat was at peace, for his God had given him rest on every side" (2 Chron. 20:30, NIV). This was the kind of rest I asked for and needed for Alex's journey to the uncertain; rest on every side.

"And the Lord gave them rest on every side, just as he had solemnly promised their ancestors. None of their enemies could stand against them, for the Lord helped them conquer all their enemies" (Josh. 21:44, NLT).

I reminded God, (as though he needed it), how Rick and I were obedient to sacrifice so much and move away from my children to Germany. I asked God to honor this and give me total rest when it came to my family. I did have rest regarding my family, with the exception of Alex. God reminded me once again why he had granted me insight and revelation from these dreams pertaining to Alex. I needed them as reminders for each passing day.

The enemy was relentless, and when I would wake up and have this unrest, I did what God said to do; I continued worshipping him and soon my spirit and mind were at rest. Even when rest settled over my spirit, I did not stop praying specifically.

During this process, I journaled: "Fight for him, Lord. Step in and remove all other applicants, workers, and open the doors for him. Lord, he has gone out, day-after-day, looking for work and each day is more discouraging than the last. He's done all he can and knows to do. He is young, immature, fresh out of college, and unsure how to proceed. He feels no rest, is alone, and when he feels no rest, neither do I."

My prayers increased with more specificity: "Lord, how much longer will it take you to act? Lord, there is always a guarantee with you because we are your children. Lord, step in and may the employers pick up their phone and call Alex to work even though they may have no intentions of doing so. Lord, it appears impossible, but with you nothing is impossible, absolutely nothing (Luke 18:27). In a world where jobs are few, God, you own all and all is yours. Alex is yours, take care of him Lord."

Of greatest importance was my children's salvation, and I included this in my daily prayers over their lives. "Lord, bless my children abundantly. Bless them with a heart to seek after you and be men of integrity. Cover them with your anointing. Lord, I know what it is like to serve you wholeheartedly yet follow after my own desires. Lord, we all sin and we all have fallen short of your glory, yet you give us the free gift of your Son. You love us and you come to our defense and you protect us. Do this on behalf of Alex and Jacob. I praise your holy name."

Another week went by, and Alex still had no job, no calls, no offers. It was time to move on. He got back in his car with all his few belongings and was on his way to New Orleans.

Initially, I felt New Orleans was the place for him, but when he set off for Shriever I felt peace knowing it wasn't Texas. I knew Alex was going in the direction God had prepared all along. God was giving me the rest I needed in answers to my worship and prayers.

At first I had no idea why God sent Alex to Shriever, but in the process Alex was learning what it meant to rely solely on God. Not on his parents, not in his own strength and plans, but God's.

"For the Lord is good to all those who seek him and follow his ways. Make it clear, Lord, the way you want Alex to go. Whatever you desire of him, you will complete. How exciting to be in your will, especially when it comes to doing the impossible and knowing only God can perform and complete his commands," I journaled.

The majority of my praise and thanks were for the miracles we had already seen. They were of great comfort and a reminder of how God was orchestrating every detail for Alex's well-being.

I praised God for Jacob's growth in the Lord. During this process Jacob called to tell me he was praying our family verse (Ps. 32:8), but also asked what additional verses we learned each morning during his childhood before they got on the school bus.

It's a small thing, but this was a glimmer of hope how God's Word never returns void. Only God can give this kind of desire. God used Jacob to minister to Alex in what appeared to be a simple way, but for me, it provided rest in a big way. I continued to speak in faith that no matter the employers in New Orleans, God would fight for Alex's position. God, in his faithfulness, spoke again to guide and direct with amazing clarity. There was nothing to question, because God's words were precise.

"God's voice is heard by those who meet with him in secret prayer. God is very careful to whom he speaks. It is only to those who value his voice so much that they shut out the whole world to get alone and wait for him" (Wilkerson, 2014, World Challenge).

Part 7

Breathtaking Miracles

9

A Son's Passage, A Mother's Responsibility

Get Out of Bed!

"But you, lazybones, how long will you sleep?
When will you wake up?" (Prov. 6:9, NLT).

Continuing to wait for answers to our prayers for Alex's career, I went to bed one night just like any other and woke up abruptly from a deep sleep at 3:45 a.m. It would have been easy to dismiss this as insomnia or a bad dream or a sudden thought, but I knew God wanted me up. Selfishly, I laid in bed and prayed for everyone and everything I could think of. I wanted to pray the easy way, comfortably in my bed, with hopes of falling back to sleep.

I am nobody special, but I do know a vibrant prayer life opens the windows of my heart to recognize when God is embracing me personally. God kept nudging me. I know because it is the same spiritual sense that I had during my *Celestial Vision*.

God was present, no audible words, but there was no doubt it was him. In my heart I had this tug, an urgency to get out of bed, and read a specific story in the Bible. So often God's voice is a nudge, that nagging feeling that won't go away.

"But make sure that you don't get so absorbed and exhausted in taking care of all your day-by-day obligations that you lose track of the time and doze off, oblivious to God. The night is about over, dawn is about to break. Be up and awake to what God is doing! God is putting the finishing touches on the salvation work he began when we first believed. We can't afford to waste a minute, must not squander these precious daylight hours in frivolity and indulgence, in sleeping around and dissipation, in bickering and grabbing everything in sight. Get out of bed and get dressed! Don't loiter and linger, waiting until the very last minute. Dress yourselves in Christ, and be up and about!" (Rom. 13:11–14, MSG).

It was the account when Jesus appeared to the disciples after the crucifixion and before his ascension. Despite hearing God's instructions, I initially attempted to do things my way. I tried to convince myself praying in bed was good enough. Had I kept lying there I would have settled for less, not an abundance of God's grace and direction. I would not have experienced another miracle. A reminder of his promises that he answers generously.

The longer I lay in bed, the more intense the push to get up came. Forty-five minutes later, at 4:30 a.m., I reluctantly dragged myself out of bed. I turned the kitchen light on, grabbed my computer and searched for this account in the Bible. I turned to John 21 and with my eyes half closed, I said a little prayer asking God to show me why these passages were so important.

When I opened to John 21, God nudged my spirit to start with chapter 20. As I was reading chapter 20 and the story of "doubting Thomas," Jesus said "stop doubting and believe." When I read this I had to repent. No matter how many times God was guiding and making things known for my son's future, there were still moments of doubt. Like Thomas, I couldn't see what was taking place.

When I got to verse 19, I had another impression and was listening intently for God to speak. "On the evening of the first day of the week, when the disciples were together, with the doors locked for fear of the Jewish leaders, Jesus came and stood among them and said, 'Peace be with you!'"

"The doors were locked."

My *Lockers Keys and Dream*, I journaled, was assurance from my heavenly father that he was stepping in on Alex's behalf, walking through closed doors at this time. This revelation was a guide to pray specifically for God to go before Alex and open doors. It was clear what the keys in the dream represented. God was "taking" the keys and preparing to open doors for Alex.

If I had it my way, I would do the planning and organizing and there would be no room for God to work a miracle. Had I tried to figure things out for Alex, remained in the habit of doing things my way, I would not have allowed God to exhibit his unending love over my son's life.

I never could have imagined how God would miraculously clear the way for my son. Even though I was waiting with expectation for God to move on Alex's behalf, I could never have anticipated how he would bring about the miracle my son so desperately needed. How God lovingly exhibited his greatness because his love is beyond understanding.

"Thank you God for getting me out of bed, confirming the purpose of the keys in the dream, which represented the time God would open doors for employment." I prayed in the early morning hours. I had no idea this was the beginning of greater miracles stemming from the early morning hours from simply getting out of bed when God said to do so.

I continued reading.

"Suddenly an angel shook him awake and said,
'Get up and eat'" (1 Kings 19:5, MSG).

Miracle in Numbers, Again!

"… Jesus spoke to them: 'Good morning! Did you catch anything for breakfast?' They answered, 'No.' he said, 'Throw the net off the right side of the boat and see what happens.' They did what he said. All of a sudden there were so many fish in it, they weren't strong enough to

pull it in. Then the disciple Jesus loved said to Peter, 'It's the Master!'
When Simon Peter realized that it was the Master, he threw on some
clothes, for he was stripped for work, and dove into the sea. The other
disciples came in by boat for they weren't far from land, a hundred
yards or so, pulling along the net full of fish. When they got out of the
boat, they saw a fire laid, with fish and bread cooking on it. Jesus said,
'Bring some of the fish you've just caught.' Simon Peter joined them and
pulled the net to shore—153 big fish. And even with all those fish, the
net didn't rip. Jesus said, 'Breakfast is ready'" (John 21: 21, MSG).

God is in the Matrix of Technology

I finished chapter 20 and continued to Chapter 21. I stopped at
"Afterwards ..." I wasn't sure if and how it was significant and continued praying for God to reveal what I wasn't seeing. As I sat there in
the early morning hours, the number of fish lifted off the pages and
my eyes remained fixed on the number.

I said a quick prayer and asked God to show me why the number of fish were relevant and what they represented. God reminded
me how important numbers are, as he had faithfully proven from
709, 84, and 3467.

The disciples were obedient and did as Jesus told them to.
Because of their faith, they caught an abundant supply of fish (153
large fish to be exact) and could barely pull their nets in. With the
number 153 staring me in the face, I did the only thing I could
think of at 4:30 in the morning. I did the usual when I don't have an
answer. I go to the Internet.

I Google just about everything, so I figured why not in this
instance. I chose to search the number and Alex's career. It was too
early to reason how absurd it sounded. I typed in the search engine,
"153 commercial diving."

What I saw before me astonished me. The first link was the
United States government's website titled: Article 153. Commercial

Diving Operations. The U.S. government's general industry standards for commercial diving is found in Article 153.

God had taken my breath away, again, and tears began running down my face, breathless, thinking "*Wow*, God. *Wow, wow, wow!*" If there are any doubters and you are like me, the need to see to believe, go to this link: http://www.dir.ca.gov/title8/sb7g26a153apb.html.

For the number of fish to be the same as the article for the career in which Alex was trying to find a job was miraculous. The unimaginable had become indescribable. This was another miracle for me that this information sprung up first from billions of other potential options. I can't make this stuff up. God is amazing!

God created numbers, and they are specific. Numbers with God in dreams are important. In the Bible God gives numbers of tribes, armies, days, events. I don't find where God uses the words *approximately*. Such was the case with the number of fish. Each time a number is referenced in the Bible, it is exact and for a specific purpose. Numbers in the Bible reinforce God's perfect Word and precision.

God continually endorsed Alex's career and we had this to shout about. Man may try to dispute God's mighty hand over my son's life, but this was an absolutely verifiable miracle that could be validated to those who doubt God's supernatural power. Alex was in the center of God's process. What love!

"I'm giving you something to boast in. Boast in who I am. Share with others. Don't hesitate," God kept reaffirming. The process on this early morning was God going before Alex, opening doors in the field he went to school for. *Wow!*

During those moments of unrest, God gave specific reassurance along the way to bring complete rest and tranquility for what I did not see. I continued to thank God for all he had done and was doing and his goodness and love for my son and our family.

"Wherever you walk, they'll guide you; whenever you rest, they'll guard you; when you wake up, they'll tell you what's next. For sound advice is a beacon, good teaching is a light …" (Prov. 6:22–23, MSG).

The Clock Keeps Ticking

Purpose and Promises in Numbers

"My counsel is this: Live freely, animated and motivated by God's Spirit. Then you won't feed the compulsions of selfishness. For there is a root of sinful self-interest in us that is at odds with a free spirit, just as the free spirit is incompatible with selfishness. These two ways of life are antithetical, so that you cannot live at times one way and at times another way according to how you feel on any given day. Why don't you choose to be led by the Spirit?" (Gal. 5:16–18, MSG).

Another abrupt wake-up at 3:45 a.m. It was the second time in two weeks God was waking me up in the wee hours of the morning. Even though I had previously experienced words of comfort and *wow*-miracles, I remained comfortably in my bed. I preferred succumbing to my selfish desires—sleep.

God was tugging at my head and heart to get up and read John 21, again. As soon as I went through my list of people to pray for, it was time to get out of bed. I would try to do so with enthusiasm even though my mind and body signals were saying, "sleep." I am thankful that my God never condemned, but showed endless patience, as was evident by his waiting for me to get out of bed.

As I was opening my Bible to John 20 and 21, God nudged me to start where I left off the previous morning in my devotions. I was reading in the book of Ezra, which begins with the lineage and specific numbers of how many were in certain tribes (e.g., Levites).

Even though I know every word in the Bible is there for a reason, I must admit I often skim over these sections because they don't seem relevant, and frankly, I find them boring to read. Here I was, sleeping soundly and I got a God wake-up call to read something that would normally cure insomnia.

It was evident that God's hand was directing every detail of our lives and especially Alex's at this point along life's journey. On this morning, however, I paid more attention to see if I could determine how numbers symbolically help interpret dreams. God woke me up to focus on numbers and numbers only.

The story of Gideon in Judges not only describes how angels came and sat with him, (Judg. 6:13) but also how his army was reduced to 22,000, and again to 10,000, and finally to an army of 300. God is very specific (Judg. 7:3, NLT).

I don't like the thought that God would give me less of what I think I need to win battles. What God continues to impress upon my heart is "if I don't put myself in a position to receive miracles, I won't see and experience miracles." I want to be like Gideon. When God tells me to operate with less, it's so God can work miracles and people will look on and say, "Wow, who did that? My God, that's who!"

I was now awake, eyes wide open, without the help of caffeine. Through the same scripture I had previously found boring, God was revealing his well-defined plan through the tiniest of details. What appeared irrelevant and mundane was another beautiful illustration of how meticulous God is when directing each step along life's journey.

Finding rest during the waiting was something I was seeking daily. What I discovered was how God was using this simple wake-up call to bring calm in my spirit yet again. Journaling these miracles and receiving a new word kept my focus on God, not in the waiting and wondering, and what I considered delays.

At the same time God was teaching me another way I insult him is by minimizing his sovereignty and answers to prayers as happenstance, opposed to miracles. Reading Ezra is a simple example of how the Word of God confirms and brings comfort. God knew I needed rest and gave it in yet another way that took little effort. He simply asked me to get out of bed.

IF I DON'T PUT MYSELF IN A POSITION TO RECEIVE MIRACLES, I WILL NEVER SEE MIRACLES.

I find it interesting how God kept waking me up at the same time—3:45 a.m. It's during this time in the night where I have my deepest sleep. My mind is truly resting and I'm not running through every detail of the day and the following day. I love how God speaks into my spirit when my mind and body are still and I cannot interrupt. He wanted my full attention and he got it.

"God's loyal love couldn't have run out, his merciful love couldn't have dried up. They're created new every morning. How great your faithfulness! I'm sticking with God [I say it over and over]" (Lam. 3:22–24, MSG).

Lockers Sealed

Alex set out each morning knocking on doors, looking for work. One organization interviewed him immediately upon showing up, but said they weren't hiring. Nevertheless, the gentlemen handed him his business card as well as a friend's, who was hiring on the other side of town. He set off in another direction, hoping for an interview.

The second gentlemen did the same, giving him his contact information, but this time they said they would check Alex's references. It had been three months since he left Georgia and this was the first word of encouragement for employment.

During this informal interview, the gentlemen made it clear there were two certifications he didn't have and it wasn't his practice to hire anyone without those qualifications. However, upon hearing this, immediately God revealed the *Lockers and Keys Dream* and clarity about how to keep praying.

I voiced to God that only he could open the door regardless of their job vacancies and even if Alex was lacking certifications. I prayed the company would get rid of the slackers and see the need to hire a hard worker, specifically my son.

I continued to come boldly to God's throne, ask for anything, and so I did. "Be the kind of woman who, when your feet hit the floor in the morning, the Devil says, 'Oh no, she's up'" (Author Unknown). I hope I can be this kind of woman one day.

God revealed the two lockers represented both companies and their business cards. Immediately the burden to intercede was released. No person or situation could stop what God was doing. I rejoiced, thanking God for moving heaven and earth on my son's behalf. I hadn't seen how this would come about, but the dreams to intercede reaffirmed the time was now.

No matter how many miracles and answered prayers we received, the enemy was relentless, continually throwing doubt and confusion. The *Black Pearls Dream* surfaced again and I recognized immediately how the enemy was trying to *choke"=* me to unbelief. Instead, I thanked and praised God, which helped to not linger on negative and anxious thoughts. Immediately the weight of doubt and fear dissipated. I was able to breathe again.

"Pray in the Spirit at all times and on every occasion. Stay alert and be persistent in your prayers" (Eph. 6:18, NLT).

Where the enemy tried to distract, God reminded me of the latter part of the *Black Pearls Dream*: "baby." God was birthing something new, confirmed from two dreams. "Pregnancy" from the first dream connected to this dream and symbolizing the birth and delivery of something beautiful.

I referred many times to what God had already done. God had manifested himself in a variety of ways, exhibiting his continuous love and miraculous wonders. We were close to another miracle, the miracle of a job, and the enemy wasn't wasting time.

Each step we recognized God's sovereignty and control at every crossing along the journey. Where the devil tried to manipulate, God skillfully managed.

Why is the offer of a job a miracle? I believe because we allowed God to guide our steps, waited for him to orchestrate every detail, which stemmed from prayer. God says to pray continually, about all things, and we did.

WHERE THE DEVIL TRIES TO MANIPULATE,
GOD SKILLFULLY MANAGES.

God Doesn't Sleep

"If you wake me each morning with the sound of your loving voice,
I'll go to sleep each night trusting in you. Point out the road I must
travel; I'm all ears, all eyes before you" (Ps.143:7–10, MSG).

"'How can you sleep at a time like this?' he shouted.
'Get up and pray to your god!'" (Jon. 1:6, NLT).

Rise and shine! Again? Two weeks later, 3:45 a.m. again, but this time I didn't hesitate and sprang out of bed enthusiastically. If there was a new word, a new prayer strategy, I wanted to know what it was. The timing wasn't convenient, but God's timing is perfect.

I sat at my kitchen table with a greater expectation because God had done so much in the early morning hours through familiar scripture. I began to read with an intensity and eagerness I had not done previously.

God has taught me over the years to never underestimate the power of the Word through familiar scripture. God is the Word and the Word is Life, living and breathing. A reminder once again for the reason God has instructed me to include Biblical verses in this book.

Ask me the question again, "How did I know what God was saying? *Every* step was supported and reaffirmed in scripture."

After I reread John chapter 20, I stopped at the passage where the disciples were meeting behind closed and locked doors. When I read, "Suddenly, Jesus was standing there among them…" it dawned on me the open door in the dream where the keys were hanging, was symbolic that God doesn't need keys to open doors and create a job for Alex. He makes a way for all things. God was revealing something new from this section of scripture. He was filling me with peace and confirming he doesn't need keys and the time was imminent. There are no closed doors with God and he was continuing to go before Alex.

God's extraordinary goodness didn't stop that morning. I focused once more on Thomas. I had previously repented for doubting what I could not see. This time it was different. Thomas wasn't in the room when Jesus appeared.

When Jesus walked in he said, "Peace be with you." Thomas wasn't present to hear these beautiful words of comfort. For Alex, God was walking through closed doors, unseen, telling me the same "peace be with you." I wonder, had Thomas been present would he be referred to as "doubting Thomas" for the next two thousand years?

What I love about this account in the Bible is when Thomas did come into the room, Thomas had a personal conversation with Jesus, who took time just for him to show him what he needed to believe. Again, what love God has for each of us, for me, for my children.

I continued on to John chapter 21, back to the account where Jesus told them to cast their nets, but now, something new stood out. Jesus told the disciples to cast their net on the "other side." "Lord, show this company it is time to 'cast their net to the other side' and hire someone less qualified and do something different in their hiring practices," I prayed. This was another directive God was providing on how to pray as he continued to create the path along this journey.

Lack of qualifications were immaterial to God and I believed this was God's master plan all along. God was providing a new tactic to our prayers. The longer we waited, the more promises he gave, which ultimately gave us more to boast in him and to share with others. I have no doubt God loves to guide our steps, literally, when we wait patiently and with expectation.

Alex arrived at the docks as the company opened, prepared to give his speech as to why they should hire him. The supervisor who interviewed him was talking with two individuals. He looked at Alex and said, "You know what, I'm going to take a chance on you. Come back at 8:30 to fill out paper work and go do a drug test later in the day." Only God!

God displayed his mighty hand more than we could ever have imagined. When Alex graduated from the diving academy he had several certifications. However, upon hiring, Alex was told he would have additional training and certifications. Once again, God brought to light a part of a dream (what the keys symbolized) I vaguely remembered.

Miracle after miracle took place through prayer and an openness to listen and look for God to work through many different methods. God was forever faithful through our steps of obedience. God always came through and in abundance, the way he always does. When I have "ears to hear," I recognize God speaks again and again.

It was a journey of trust for me as much as it was for Alex. We have so much to boast in God's love. Through prayer and believing, God lovingly, gently, and perfectly prepared a path for Alex. God had everything under control, he just needed to ensure we were too.

"… The Spirit of the Lord gave them rest. You led your people, Lord, and gained a magnificent reputation" (Isa. 63:10, NLT).

Everything Should Depend on God

"Pray as though everything depended on God. Work as though everything depended on you" (Saint Augustine).

God promises his Words will never go void and he is faithful to his Word, always. I continued praying Alex would be bold in his faith. In time, God prepared Alex's heart to hear him personally. Over the course of a year, Alex called to share his beautiful encounter with God.

"I know this sounds crazy, but God used New Orleans to help me find myself and to appreciate who God is. God never left me and through his patience he revealed his love through a whisper. To tell me he was near and loves me. I now recognize how much he loves me and it's that love I want to share with others. I recognize those around me who don't know God and they need love, prayers, and not religious jargon," he said.

Alex had to stake a claim on his own faith before he could do something with it. The story of his testimony is long, but it's because God's process took time. Though Alex went through some of his darkest days as a young man after graduating high school, through perseverance and patience, he continued trusting in what he couldn't see. His trust in God grew because he knew there was only One who could orchestrate the events in his life so beautifully.

During what appeared to be many delays, God encouraged us to remain focused on him and give him the glory along the way for what he wills, can, does, and did for Alex. Alex has much to boast of in the glory of God, because he walked his own journey and discovered God in a more intimate way. He has his own God-story.

"Stalwart walks in step with God; his path blazed by God, he's happy. If he stumbles, he's not down for long; God has a grip on his hand" (Ps. 37:23, MSG). Praise God for his patience during times we willingly take detours outside of God's pathway.

I hate to admit how my human frailty surfaced far too often as we waited for answered prayers along Alex's journey. Thankfully, God's love is vast and his words guided and nourished my soul. God gave me the physical and mental rest I desperately needed. The process of learning to wait patiently and expectantly for God's future plans for my son, while relying on God's methods resulted in total rest and peace, but it came only from a daily process of seeking God.

The Lord moved heaven and earth on Alex's behalf and I will continue to express my gratitude at the wonders God performed. For my children in general, their spiritual journeys are another example of God's glory and tenderness, of his love when we cherish his friendship.

I will not be silenced and shroud God's wonders deep within the recesses of my mind and heart. God is too good for me to remain speechless.

> *"At day's end I'm ready for sound sleep, For you, God, have put my life back together" (Ps. 4:8, MSG).*

Part 8

Angels and Images

10

Awareness of Angels

"But to which of the angels has he ever said, 'Sit at my right hand until I make Your enemies a footstool for your feet?' Are they not all ministering spirits, sent out to render service for the sake of those who will inherit salvation!" (Heb. 1:13–14 MSG).

Initially I questioned whether or not I should include the word *angel* in the title of this section. As far as I know, all my Christian friends believe in angels, the devil and his demons, spirit-beings. However, few refer to how God uses his angels. Fewer still have seen God's glory displayed through one of his heavenly creations.

Hebrews says the angels are servants to the children of God. "The angels perform the word of God that is proclaimed by the voice of the Lord. God's angels become the agents of change whenever prophecies require events to be altered, things to be accomplished or wars to be won. The angels are the ones who are commissioned to carry out this type of prophecy" (Vallotton, 2007).

Years ago, I had a conversation with a coworker and she told me that she does not believe hell is eternal, but heaven is. "Hell is a metaphor for the devil's existence, but not a place," she said. What we agreed upon is the devil and his demons are real, just like God and his angels. I could not convince her the definition of the words eternity and eternal are the same for heaven and for hell. Matthew

25:46 states, "Then they will go away to eternal punishment, but the righteous to eternal life" (NIV).

I found the same to be true when defining angels and demons. There was a definite difference among the Christian community of how we view the devil and his army of demons and God's angels. I have noticed that the body of Christ frequently gives warnings to be aware of the devil, his demons, and unseen evil forces in the world. However, there is a peculiar silence in the Church when it comes to conversations about angels. What I find more interesting is the majority of Bible verses quoted in Christian circles pertain to the devil, not God's angels. Upon honest reflection, I found I am guilty of the same.

I want to discern when the devil is near, but I prefer to have my spirit quickened to God's angelic spirit-beings. I want to understand the goodness of his army and how he sends them to do his will and intervene in the affairs of men.

The Bible records numerous accounts where people were confronted by an angel to bring God's words of encouragement, warning, or direction. When Jesus was praying at the Mount of Olives, "an angel from heaven appeared to him and strengthened him" (John 22:43, NIV).

Having an awareness of angels isn't to put them above God, but it is to recognize they are from God. Angels are sent from God's Holy Throne and it is no wonder when one stands in the presence of angels they are fearful.

How could one not be overwhelmed when a spiritual being is sent directly from the throne of God Almighty! If we are willing to accept that we can discern an evil presence, should we not be more attuned to God's heavenly presence?

The Bible tells us to pray for discernment (Phil. 1:9–10) and this is not only to know when the enemy is lurking, but for us to understand how God is working supernaturally in our lives with his heavenly messengers (Ps. 119:125).

The Bible cautions us not to worship angels (created), instead of the Creator (God himself). It is unbiblical to do so and I would not call on angels to do my bidding. However, I am open for God to send his angels to do my bidding on my behalf if he so chooses.

Unfortunately, discussing angels comes with controversy in the church. I think this may stem from a fear that people will worship angels and not God. I also believe that because the world is so fixated on the supernatural, the paranormal, that Christians abandon the thought that a holy presence might actually be God sending an angel to comfort us.

For me, when I say I want all of God and for God to choose how he speaks to me, I hope he uses all his creation (i.e., friends, family, even angels).

Though controversy may arise on the subject of angels, to omit this topic would be to ignore God's creation and glory in all things. God's Word promises to teach us what is true and this may also come through his messengers. I really don't find an answer in scripture that would steer me away from acknowledging and accepting God's help through angels.

> *"For the Spirit teaches you all things, and what he teaches is true—it is not a lie. So continue in what he has taught you, and continue to live in Christ" (1 John 2:27b, NLT).*

Once again, God reminded me to raise awareness about the beauty of his character, the fact that he is love, and to know what is in heaven is available on earth.

Our family had another prayer request. After three years of living overseas, we decided we would no longer lease our home. Before the tenant moved, we made provisions to sell our home.

We tired of the challenges of leasing a home while living so far away. I had given up my career when we moved overseas and our income had become far more limited than what we had always been used to.

Daily, I would go to God in prayer asking him to immediately bring a buyer and close the sale. I often think, "I'm the most annoying child of God there is," asking for too much, too often. On the other hand, I love it when my children come to me, so our Father must love it when we come to him. It is the same with God. "… How much more will your Father who is in heaven give good things to those who ask him" (Matt. 7:10, NKJV).

While we waited each day, week, month, for our home to sell, the Lord guided me step-by-step on how to pray. I can't reiterate enough how God loves to be involved in the daily affairs of life. I had lovely mornings talking to God where he has told me, "I can and I will."

One morning, without previous experience and understanding of how God uses angels, the Lord sketched into my mind how his presence was over me. Once more God asked me to stand in silence and wait upon him. It reminded me of Ezekiel, "It [an angel] said, 'Son of man, stand up. I have something to say to you'" (Ezek. 2:1, MSG). I wanted to hear what God had to say.

I stood in silence with my eyes closed and within seconds I had an image before me of two angels standing on both sides of me. High and mighty, lifted far above my head, their wings gently swaying. This image was beautiful and beyond description. I consider this to also be an "open heaven" encounter with God.

Ezekiel's "open heaven" description is found in Ezekiel 1:1 (NLT), and when he was at the river, "the heavens were opened and I saw visions of God." Another heavenly visitation of God bringing what is in heaven to earth.

Within moments, their wings moved ever so slowly until they began to engulf me, completely covering and protecting me. It was a beautiful picture how God is with me as was illustrated from the *Parachute Dream.*

I remained silent and as God's presence rested over me I saw the word "protected" above my head. A sense of calm and peace filled the room of my heart. I remained silent trying to take in the entire meaning of the image and, most of all, the experience of standing in the center of God's presence.

"For the angel of the Lord is a guard; he surrounds and defends all who fear him" (Ps. 34:7, NLT).

The word *protected* bounced overhead, back and forth, like a butterfly. While it flittered above, I was unable to focus long on the word. It's hard to explain, but it was clear the word "protected" was secondary to his presence. God's guidance for me was to remain fixated only on him.

I continued standing in silence, with my hands resting by my side when another image appeared. A second image came and God reminded me when my children were small, each night at bedtime we asked God to keep his angels on the four corners of our home, protecting us. Twenty years later, I was receiving this very image to see how God was surrounding our home, protecting our investment, and ensuring he was controlling all things. It became the visual instruction how to trust without seeing and to pray specifically for God's intervention.

The image changed a few moments later. Their wings opened like a fence surrounding our property that we were trying to sell, fitting together, leaving no gaps around our premises. Similar to the way God surrounded me from my *Parachute Dream*, he was surrounding our home.

The scene changed again and the two angels sitting in the front of our home opened their wings inward, creating a gateway to the entrance of our driveway.

When the image was gone, I realized several hours had passed in what seemed but a few moments. How could this be? In times past it was often a struggle to pray for an hour, a half hour, fifteen minutes. Time flies when I am in God's presence: his thoughts become mine and my time becomes his.

Like Job, I heard a voice and waited in silence. "The spirit stopped, but I couldn't see its shape. There was a form before my eyes. In the silence I heard a voice ..." (Job 4:16, NLT).

I knew how to pray for our home to sell from that day forward from this image. "God give your Word of instruction to your angels to do the bidding on our behalf. May the buyer walk through your glory as they enter the gates of our home. Your glory surrounds our home and may all who enter recognize your presence and peace over the property. May the buyer's eyes see all that is good," I prayed.

I continued to outline what God had revealed as the blueprint to include the operation of the Trinity. Receiving no offer and living so far away, these images were a constant source of peace that God was in the details.

God was stirring something new and creating within me a deeper awareness of his presence, which kept my mind fixed on him, not the clock ticking or the calendar or the routines of the day. It was a time of being submerged into God's presence, where the hours in worship and praise passed so quickly.

"For who in all of heaven can compare with the Lord? What mightiest angel is anything like the Lord? The highest angelic powers stand in awe of God. He is far more awesome than all who surround his throne. O Lord God of heaven's Armies! Where is there anyone as mighty as you, O Lord? You are entirely faithful" (Ps. 89:6–8, NLT).

Exhaustless Prayer

"Exhaustless possibilities of prayer … prayer is a mighty force; prayers of saints are a perceptual force; shorn (past)—prayer has been shorn of its simplicity; its majesty, and its power. God still lives, and miracles still live while God lives and acts, for miracles are God's ways of acting …" (Bounds and Murray, n.d.).

I know God doesn't want me to settle for yesterday's blessings, but to live a life of expectancy each day of how his mighty wonders can extend over every part of my life.

God's Word says, "His mercies are new every morning." I wake up rejuvenated when I think of this promise. God's love is endless and in recent days he has spoken into my spirit a new prayer, "Lord, you are a God of infinite character, therefore, I want to see you in a new way." And, I believe, it is in God's nature to want me to see him anew.

There is no way to explain searching for the deeper things of God, other than to state that through prayer, God awakens me to seek his infinite goodness. God says those who know him are taught by the Spirit and the Spirit of God explains spiritual things (1 Cor. 2:13). God freely gives and I freely and willingly receive.

> *"God's Spirit searches out everything and shows us even God's deep secrets ... no one can know God's thoughts except God's own Spirit. And God has actually given us his spirit [not the world's spirit] so we can know the wonderful things God has freely given us," (1 Cor. 2:10–12, NLT).*

God's ways are infinite and the more I know him, I don't have to question or shy away from experiencing him display an extravaganza of his presence. He wants me to see and recognize him in all his fullness and to share with others what he has done. God's goodness is never ending and it is his nature to do good things for me and you.

As my spiritual journey through worship and prayer continued, it is here I saw more of God's splendor. Seeing God in his fullness is an experience of his great love. When I see what he wants me to see there is life and power and it is how my trust in him increases. I begin to understand what "exhaustless possibilities" of prayer means and can look like.

God's Word says to keep my eyes open for him and if my eyes are open I will see him and, without question, hear him. Being in the center of God's presence increases not only a familiarity to his voice, but a comfortable peace with the unknown and unexplainable. It's what creates a continued hunger for more of God.

"I crave your presence, Lord. Make me continually love sick for you. Help me to sleep less so I can be in your presence" was a journal entry from 2006. God never stops teaching, and I am grateful and eager to learn.

> *"Hallelujah! Thank God! Pray to him by name! Tell everyone you meet what he has done! ... translate his wonders ... you who seek God. Live a happy life! Keep your eyes open for God, watch for his*

works; be alert for signs of his presence. Remember the world of
wonders he has made, his miracles ... " (Ps. 105:1–6, MSG).

There was a freedom in knowing I was keeping the doors of my
heart open for God to reveal more of his character. For the first time,
God had given me a personal glimpse how he uses angels as his messengers. "For the message God delivered through angels has always
stood firm ..." (Heb. 2:2, NLT). The more time I took with God,
my heart was open to see more of his creation.

The nearness of God's Being flooded my soul. You can't submerge yourself in water and come out dry. "Rivers of living water will
brim and spill out of the depths of anyone who believes in me this
way" (John 7:38, MSG).

AN EXTRAVAGANZA OF GOD'S VARIETY
IS AVAILABLE TO ALL.

Coffee and Conversation

"Congenial conversation—what a pleasure! The right word
at the right time—beautiful" (Ps. 15:23, MSG).

I continued to dedicate my time and day to the Lord with a
more conscious effort to know him more intimately. I tried very
hard to keep my day consistent, starting my mornings with a cup of
coffee, worship music, and reading my Bible. My love for God, his
words, became more precious than ever. In my spirit I felt God was
saying (and still does), "Let's have a conversation."

We continued praying for the sale of our home and each passing
day my prayers turned into pleas, begging God to move. Without
providing an overabundance of details, the individual managing the
lease on our home was holding our funds long after they should have

been deposited into our bank account. It was a constant battle to obtain what was owed to us. Months would go by without payment and it became clear she was being dishonest. We were never sure when and if we would be paid. We desperately needed God to protect our finances.

During my quiet times, I never know what's going to happen with God and it could simply be to just rest and enjoy the moment with Christ through scripture. This morning, God once again placed within my spirit the need to stand in silence and with great anticipation.

Within moments, he filled the room with another illustration. God continued to reveal his character, which turned into beautiful conversations. It's my own coffee time with God the Father, God the person, God my friend. I saw a similar picture of the relationship the Son has with the Father. As I stood there, taking up the same posture from previous days, I began to see what appeared like a movie trailer, a glimpse of God holding my home.

What I saw with my spiritual eyes and understood was how Jesus does nothing outside the will of the Father. Jesus moves on our behalf when the Father gives the Word go. *Go*, meaning he would take our home, place it into the hands of Jesus and move heaven to earth on our behalf. Therefore, I began to pray, "God let go of our home and place it into the hands of Jesus. May the Son be glorified as the Holy Spirit moves over our home. You, God, will be glorified as the Holy Spirit works on our behalf, bringing glory to the Son all to bring glory to you, Father."

The illustrations from my dreams and visions (specifically the order of the *Love of the Cross, Celestial*, and *Conversation with God Visions*) were wonderful promises of how the Trinity is put into action. It was a guide for "how I can pray" and recognize the partnership of the Father, Son, and Holy Spirit working as one *(Parachute Dream)*.

I concluded that God gave me these "pictures" as another way to pray. I was seeing God on his throne and a glimpse of how a need of mine is seen and cared for by my heavenly Father. These scenes were like movie trailers; scenes in action to get me excited for what God was doing and preparing to do. "Give your word to the Son, move heaven and earth, and operate on our behalf. God, please give your word to Jesus to put the Holy Spirit into action," I prayed. They were meant to keep me vigilant in prayer and to wait with expectation for God's divine intervention.

I stand on God's Word to pray about everything. His Word says to pray continually about all things, so I did and I do. I tend to engage my voice and my body while telling stories. Sometimes I get so excited I stand up thinking it gives greater emphasis to what I'm about to share. From this beautiful scene, I talked to God in the same manner I would a friend. I put my hands into motion, acting out as though what was invisible was before me. I probably looked like I was miming, acting out what I saw before me, but with words.

Brother Lawrence recommended to develop a habit of entertaining yourself with God. "Freeing the mind will permit a comfort with God" (Lawrence, 2008). I was becoming more comfortable spending time with God in ways that were different, strange, and humorous, including through body motions that would be natural with a close friend.

The more I worshipped with my whole being (voice and body), the more comfortable I was becoming during my times with God. Over the past year God had already been teaching me the benefits of not only moving my lips, but my body. I don't think God wants me to worship and pray like a ventriloquist, words only and lifeless.

I cupped my hands as though I were *holding* my home the way I saw God doing. Again, there is something powerful taking place in the spirit when I express my prayers through physical actions. There is no doubt when God imparts a message into my conscious, he is moving supernaturally.

Daily, I asked, "God, please do it today, now." In respect to God, I would repent for my boldness and it didn't last long because then I would boldly say to God, "But you tell us we can come to you honestly." I was like a child continually, saying, "But referring back to what the Word of God says, you told me so, you said I could."

The beautiful life of Gideon continued to speak to me. Gideon prayed boldly and honestly. In Judges 6, three times Gideon asked God to prove the Lord was with him. In verse 17, he says to God, "Show me a sign to prove that it is really the Lord speaking to me." And then in verse 36 he responds to God, "If you are truly going to use me to rescue Israel as your promise, prove it to me …" And Gideon continued with some instructions. God answered his prayer, and I love verse 39 because Gideon apparently needed more assurance and made another request to God, "Please don't be angry with me, but let me make one more request." God answered every time, assuring Gideon God was going with him. I want to be like Gideon.

Because God's nature is loving and encouraging, I have this sense of him smiling down on me, possibly thinking, "Here she goes again." God has never rebuked me for coming to him and asking. The Bible has many examples of bold prayers and I love Gideon's boldness: "If you are truly going to use me…prove it to me in this way" (Judg. 6:17, NLT).

I continued to see God sitting solemnly on his throne, Jesus never leaving his side, and they were in communication with the Father. I wondered what it meant for God to sit solemnly on his throne.

As I observed this beautiful yet personal image between the Father and Son, it was as though they were having their "coffee time," conversing with one another and I was their topic of discussion. Not only was Jesus interceding on my behalf, he was exhibiting how he does nothing outside the will of his heavenly Father and for all glory to be given to the Father.

> *"Christ Jesus died for us and was raised to life for us,*
> *and he is sitting in the place of honor at God's right*
> *hand, pleading for us" (Rom. 8:34, NLT).*

Previously, I had seen God sitting solemn with an unreadable presence. Now I understood his silence, sitting solemnly, is how patience looks. Over time, I understood a bit more of his sovereignty, his control in all things, his Love. In 1 Corinthians 13, the *first attribute of love is patience.* God is the essence of love and it was this love; God working on our behalf.

It was through this process my journey remained on the road to worship. I not only trusted the Word that says he will do this, I looked for God to show me how he was doing this and how he wanted me to actively participate.

I wanted to see the image of God and our home before me day-after-day change. I petitioned God to stretch out his arms to sell my home. Daily I displayed and verbalized what I wanted the hand of God to do. I wanted God to respond the way he did for Moses when he stretched out his staff to part the Red Sea.

"Do that for me, God. Stretch your arm from the heavens to Jesus, who in turn will stretch his arm and place my home into the hands of the Holy Spirit—putting the Holy Spirit into action," I prayed. I was seeing the movements of heaven to earth.

This vision of the Trinity, working as one, gave me much confidence as to what Jesus promised when he descended to heaven after the crucifixion: "But when the helper (Holy Spirit) comes, whom I shall send to you from the Father, the Spirit of truth who proceeds from the Father, he will testify of Me" (John 15:26, MSG).

A week or so after the movie trailer revelation and my continued request to God to "let go" of our home, I was given a beautiful update to the image God was showing me. I saw God gently lowering my home into the hands of Jesus.

Day after day, I prayed over the checklist of items that needed to fall in place to finalize the sale of our home. Our buyer needed to accept the offer of their buyer for their home. Both of our homes needed inspections, loan approvals before we could have the documents finalized.

Anyone who has bought or sold a home understands the variables that need to be factored in and aligned before the sale and title documents can be signed. I prayed continually over each requirement.

Another morning with God, praying over the required items to close, I got excited and stood in my kitchen. I cupped my hands as though they were holding my home. I walked in a line, placing my home over every detail, envisioning the process and particulars that needed orchestrated to sell our home—basically voicing the steps, the checklist, necessary to close on our home.

"May all inspections, appraisals, every detail come to fruition from our buyer's buyer to the signing of final sale." I set my hands symbolically down over the buyer's buyer, their inspections, their bank, etc. I thanked God and believed he had taken my home out of the hands of the person managing our lease, even though she was continuing to find reasons to hold onto our funds. God was showing me—he had us in his hands—his care.

God appeared so near as though I could reach out and touch him. I know I don't always place my body in a disposition to talk to God, but I do want to pray as Jesus did. He "lifted up his eyes to heaven, and said, Father, the hour is come; glorify your Son, that your Son also may glorify you …" (John 17:1, NLT).

Going through these motions, this process focusing on the workings of the Father, Son, and Holy Spirit seemed like an excessive and dramatic way to pray. Nevertheless, I wanted to stand before God heart, mind, body, and soul. Therefore, I continued praising God for his Word going into action. I asked that he give his angels charge and instructions to see his word through for the sale of our home.

"He could have prayed with eyes closed if it had so pleased him, but his were the opened eyes of faith and love which could look into the face of God and could yet look upon all things 'round without distraction and, therefore, it was not necessary for him to draw down the curtains of his eyelids, but he gazed into the opened heaven" (Spurgeon, n.d., Sermon #1465A).

Learning to worship naturally and effortlessly is how God opened my eyes and what it means when I sing the song, "I want to see you." Once again, if someone were watching they may think

I was hallucinating, seeing things they could not see. It was no different than when the fire of God burned and penetrated my soul. Though invisible, there was a tangible manifestation of the Holy Spirit to see as he sees.

Many of us stand in auditoriums full of people singing a chorus saying, "I want to see you," but how many of us are willing to put in the time to prepare for such a supernatural experience? If I sing "I want to see you," then I should be prepared to do so.

Lifting my eyes to heaven in worship increased my love and joy about what the cross represents. My spiritual journey included continued acknowledgment of God sitting on his throne, High and Mighty, King of kings, and Lord of all.

God's love engulfed me because I not only *believed* his promise that "his mercies are new every morning" (Ps. 119:77, NLT), but I expected to see him in all his fullness each morning.

God is remarkably generous, and I can see him anew each day. From all these experiences his presence is like the wind. You can feel the breeze even though it is invisible.

When we were in Ireland, standing atop the Cliffs of Moher, the wind from the ocean was so intense we could not stand with our feet firmly planted on the ground. For safety reasons, we had to hold onto the rail. The wind was so strong my hair was literally, and I mean literally, standing straight up, far above my head. When I wanted to "ride the wind," I let go of the rail and let the wind push me down the path.

In many ways, God has done this same thing when I'm willing to let go of norms and human expectations about how he wants to move in my life. I let go, and he pushes me beyond my current understanding of how he operates into something completely supernatural—and yes, why does this surprise me? He, who put his hand over Moses in the cleft of the rock (Exodus 33:22) is the same God who meets with me every morning!

"Look at me. I stand at the door. I knock. If you hear me call and open the door, I'll come right in and sit down to supper with you. Conquerors

will sit alongside me at the head table, just as I, having conquered, took the place of honor at the side of my Father. That's my gift to the conquerors! "Are your ears awake? Listen. Listen to the Wind Words, the Spirit blowing through the churches" (Rev. 3:19–22, MSG).

In Revelation, John speaks to the church in Laodicea and their stagnant Christianity, neither hot nor cold, but indifferent, passive, when it came to God. Over the years I focused primarily on verse 20 when Jesus accepts us (comes in and eats with us) the way we are. We only have to open the door to him.

We don't have to change before we ask him into our heart, but the beauty is that once we receive his grace and forgiveness, he can begin helping us to reflect upon his character.

I fear my words will fail to convey how simple worship leads to a beautiful picture of the approachability, yet magnificence and immense love of God, pouring over every detail of our lives. The beauty of gazing upon his Being was not only of his glory, but also the awe of God's willingness to reveal his splendor, sitting majestically on his throne.

It's his gift to sit with me. The criteria and prerequisite is to remove distractions, focus on him, and open my ears. "Listen, listen, listen to the wind of his words, pay attention to when the Spirit is blowing" (Rev. 2:17, MSG).

I realize I describe it as a new experience several times, but that's exactly how God wanted me to take delight in him and to expect a fresh experience and knowledge of his presence. Every day with Jesus is unique. Just like every sunset is new and fresh, God's qualities are endless; therefore, so are the encounters that we can have with him! This was yet another indelible experience where God pointed the way in an entirely new manner.

A short time after I experienced this vision, seeing God hand over my house to Jesus, God spoke in an unexpected way. After several days of pleading to God to move heaven and earth to protect our investment and sell our home, I awoke after having a dream of a classroom. I shared my dream with Rick and he looked at me and said he too had a dream of a classroom. Rick rarely, if ever, mentions dreams. Though he knows God speaks through dreams, it's not something he pays much attention to. His dream was an empty classroom, nothing written on the chalkboard and he heard a voice, "That's the end."

Our dreams complimented each other and provided a new directive on how to pray until we received answers to our prayers. I turned my prayer into a proclamation of what was forthcoming. An end to this ordeal was drawing to a close.

A few days later I was going through my morning routine of reading the Bible, prayer, and praise. "Thank you, God, we are at the end of this stage owning a home in Battle Creek, Michigan. This is the end," I voiced.

The following morning, (God's timing always astounds me), I opened my email and we received two offers on our home. The first e-mail I read was a potential buyer who wanted the option to lease to buy. The second was an official offer of sale.

As soon as I read the offers, immediately God reminded me of a dream I had several months prior where I was signing documents with a realtor (no faces, just hands) to lease our home with the option to buy. I kept this dream in the back of my mind and assumed this was God's way our home would sell.

However, when I read the request to lease to buy, anxiety immediately welled up and my heart began palpitating. It was as though the black pearls (*Black Pearls Dream*) were choking me. If God had given me this dream why was there a sense of uneasiness? Immediately, I went to prayer asking God why I had this anxiety from what should be good news. News I had been waiting months to hear.

God quickly revealed the agitation was a warning of what not to do (not to lease). I had assumed this dream was a guide about what we *should* do. Had the second offer on our home not come the same day, at the same moment, I may have taken this as God's direction, but he orchestrated both an answer (a sale) and a warning—such a complete gift of love. Just like his Word.

God made it obvious which offer to choose. "It is a great thing to have our eyes opened initially and foundationally; it is a great thing as we go along to have our eyes opened again and again to see what no one has been able to show us, what we have struggled to see and understand. And then God, sovereignly, by intervention from outside, touches our spiritual, eyes and we see. Is it not a great day when we see like that?" (Austin, 2011, Kindle book).

Though I couldn't see what was taking place with our home, God revealed his angels and the word "protected" to bring peace, patience, and a promise. I rejoiced how God gave me insight when we needed it and the assurance he was protecting our investment all along. God's great reservoir of goodness continually nourished my soul.

God continued to surround and energize my spirit with an appreciation for his unpredictability. Unpredictable because it is in this space, where I give him room to rapture and grab my heart where miracles began. It was through a desire to see God in ways I could not predict, when I began to see the wonders of God in abundance.

Prayer allows me to see with spiritual eyes; therefore, I cannot bypass prayer. I must be a praying believer and a "believing believer."

It was through a disciplined commitment to worship and prayer that increased my faith to believe what I could not see. Prayer and belief—it's illogical to think you can have one without the other and be effective. God reshaped my heart in so many ways by calling me to surrender my entire being to him during times of prayer.

Praying and believing: it's illogical to think you can have one without the other and be effective.

God continues to teach me how to anticipate an array of his presence. Paving the way for a fresh look into his goodness, a delight that is new and surprising. He comes when we have a teachable and open spirit. Do I want God to teach me? Without doubt I do! Do you?

"God has a huge reservoir in which to reach his children and reveal himself to further his kingdom ... there is an overflow of God's omnipotence if we open our hearts and not put restraints in place" (Isaiah 41:10) (Spurgeon, 2012, iTunes App).

Part 9

God-Connector

11

Tipping God's Network

God-Connectors

*"Join me in spreading the news; together let's
get the word out" (Ps. 34:3, MSG).*

*"All who were marked out for real life put their trust in God—they
honored God's Word by receiving that life. And this Message of salvation
spread like wildfire all through the region" (Acts 13:48–49, MSG).*

Malcolm Gladwell's bestselling book, *The Tipping Point,* describes the concept of "that magic moment when an idea, trend, or social behavior crosses a threshold, tips, and spreads like wildfire."

The primary premise of his book is how people are connectors by taking an unknown book or restaurant, and through the power of suggestion, create positive impact. The opinion of one can increase the popularity of a product or establishment.

Connectors take an obscure idea and through their contagious behavior have "the power to spark word-of-mouth epidemics … Connectors are social glue: they spread it" (p. 70). Popularity doesn't always happen from the opinions of experts, but simply through a Connector.

The obscure, unfamiliar is tipped when the unexpected becomes expected, where radical change is more than possibility. It is—contrary to all our expectations—a certainty (p. 14). People begin to see things differently, and something that formerly appears dull becomes something quite cool and change in social behavior takes place.

The disciples were God-Connectors. Through their relationship with God, this small band of misfits became the change by spreading the Good News of the Gospel of Jesus Christ. They were the tipping points, change-makers, to the message of Jesus Christ, which spread throughout history. "Wherever God sent them, lives and history were changed" (NLT, 1988, p.1684). Because God sent them, there was a certainty lives would be changed.

They were effective change-makers because "wonderful times of refreshment will come from the presence of the Lord" (Acts 2:37 and Acts 3:20, NLT). They were identified as Christ followers; therefore, they were able to "tip the scales" for Jesus. "Tip the scales" can also mean making something more or less likely to happen or to make someone more or less likely to succeed (thefreedictionary.com).

So how does it look to change the balance for Jesus? I do know God is reinventing my mental model of what a Christ-follower looks like. I want my love and devotion for Christ to be contagious enough for others to recognize God is not a fad that comes and goes. He never goes out of style.

He desires to keep our relationship fresh and new and encourages me with the hope that some part of me can be an agent for change in my life and community. As I allow Christ to shift the balance of my heart to his, I have the confidence I too can be an effective Christian and change-maker for the Kingdom of God.

Knowing God personally takes time. It takes time to recognize his presence and allow the Holy Spirit to pierce my heart for action and change. I want to be characterized as a God enthusiast, one who pursues God with a keen eye on the Living and only True God. God wants me to be his zealous advocate, but I can only promote what I know and experience.

Walking with Christ as my ever-present companion is how I recognize the differences of his presence and he confirms when his spirit bears witness with my spirit (Rom. 8:16, KJV). The Message version states, "God's Spirit touches our spirits and confirms who we really are. We know who he is, and we know who we are …" This is how I know God is in me and I'm in him.

I love my God-adventures and coming to him with expectation is where he tips my heart to see what was once obscure. By increasing my time with God, he uncovers my eyes and exposes more of his love and I have a heightened awareness of his glory.

God continues to teach me to keep my heart open and give him permission to step in supernaturally. By doing so, God illuminates his presence, giving insight into the things I would otherwise not see. God's Holy Word instructs us to go into all the world and tell others about his great love and what he has done for us. About the free gift we have through Jesus! When God tips my heart, it is indescribable and it's then the command to go changes to desire, "I want to go."

> *GOD'S PRESENCE IS WHAT PIERCES THE*
> *HEART FOR ACTION AND CHANGE.*

I agree with A. W. Tozer when he stated, "The difficulty with the Church now—even the Bible believing Church—is that we stop with revelation" (p. 18, The Attributes of God, Volume 1). I don't want to stop with revelation. What God reveals to me is cause to boast in him and for the ultimate purpose to bring him glory.

The disciples went everywhere preaching, the Master working right with them, validating the Message with indisputable evidence (Mark 16:15–18 and Acts 2:22). Twelve men changed the world with no automobiles, jets, or technology. They were God-connected, God-connectors. God promises to validate who he is with indisputable evidence. *Indisputable* means "unable to be challenged" (Dictionary.com).

"Let me tell you why you are here. You're here to be salt-seasoning that brings out the God-flavors of this earth. If you lose your saltiness, how will people taste godliness? You've lost your usefulness and will end up in the garbage. Here's another way to put it: You're here to be light, bringing out the God-colors in the world. God is not a secret to be kept. We're going public with this, as public as a city on a hill. If I make you light-bearers, you don't think I'm going to hide you under a bucket, do you? I'm putting you on a light stand. Now that I've put you there on a hilltop, on a light stand—shine! Keep open house; be generous with your lives. By opening up to others, you'll prompt people to open up with God, this generous Father in heaven" (Matt. 5:13–16, MSG).

One of my past time is searching e-stores for books from God's faithful messengers from centuries ago. My e-books and shelves are lined with these books.

I have seen a pattern, a theme emerging from each one. For hundreds of years the same message surfacing in the twenty-first century with the central focus: Be in God's presence.

I began writing this book a year before I uploaded Brother Lawrence's book, focused primarily on practicing the presence of God. His writings were *preaching* the cry of my heart. A man who lived from 1614 to 1691 and the message God pierced into his heart is as relevant in the twenty-first century as it was then.

I call this nothing short of a miracle and God's divine plan to guide those who are willing into all Truth. He has given me a confirmation to write what he has pierced so deeply in my spirit and the urgency to do it now. "Keep the conversation going, I want to be the most popular subject discussed among my creation," God repeatedly impressed upon my spirit.

Similar phrases and terminology from other resources lifted off the pages, including illustrations and accounts using the same Bible passages that I was using. As I looked over my journal entries ten years prior or longer, God had already begun impressing into my spirit the importance to devoting and developing more time with him.

God's message over the last decade was so similar to what others have been preaching, that I was initially concerned what I had already written may come across as plagiarizing. I decided to reference dates and comments within the margins of books and e-books, noting how "these words are in my book, my journals, similar to what I already wrote," etc. It was evident God was doing something extraordinary deep within my soul. The more I read, the more I was astonished. God was speaking the same heart-to-heart message to his children, another way to conceive how God does not change. He is the Word and his Word stands for all time.

God is connecting the souls of man to his and I believe he is tipping the scales to know his glory so we can share his glory with others. "… And there is nothing new under the sun" (Eccles. 1:9, NKJV). For Jesus doesn't change—yesterday, today, tomorrow, he's always totally himself" (Heb. 13:7–8, MSG).

God is sending a new generation of believers to those who are listening. I do not experience God's limitless wonders by *saying* I know Christ personally; it's by *walking* in relationship, hand-in-hand, and moving into action that I know him and experience his wonders.

Sharing God's personal words to me and the unexpected and unusual experiences of his presence is not for the sake of another story. God's Word breathes life. He is the never-changing being. I write because God has said "record for all generations, brag about me. I should never be kept a secret." It's about God's story, which does not change.

MAKE GOD THE MOST POPULAR SUBJECT
DISCUSSED AMONG HIS CREATION.

It is the spirit of God, his supernatural being, that transforms my inner-being with hope that I too can be a Connector. I want to remain part of the dialogue taking place in this generation and the generations to come. I want, God wants, others to look for him, to know and experience him for themselves. It is then we can move forward and see change for the Kingdom of God and the souls of man.

"Then he told them what they could expect for themselves: 'Anyone who intends to come with me has to let me lead. You're not in the driver's seat—I am. Don't run from suffering; embrace it. Follow me and I'll show you how. Self-help is no help at all. Self-sacrifice is the way, my way, to finding yourself, your true self'" (Luke 9:21–22, MSG).

Without question, a greater possessing of the Spirit of God has come from the practice of intercession. For me, intercession is what evokes a hunger for more of God. It's what makes my relationship with God personal and original. It's what drives me to embrace that which is unfamiliar. Prayer is what changes my heart and increases my love and compassion toward others.

Giving God permission to come as he chooses is how I see more of him and know him more intimately. From it, he opens my heart and eyes to discover who I am in him. I can't be a backseat driver, constantly questioning the route, the curves. I must sit back, relax, and let him choose the route and enjoy the scenery.

To boast and share the wonders of God is to advance the kingdom of God. If I settle for a little of God, I get a little of God, and others will see little of God. A life of spiritual complacency reduces the ability to be a God-connector.

When I have a little of God, I find myself digressing spiritually and away from God's presence. But as I have searched for more of him, he satisfies all my needs and desires. The result being I can't get enough of God's presence.

A LIFE OF SPIRITUAL COMPLACENCY REDUCES THE ABILITY TO BE A GOD-CONNECTOR.

If there is one thing God continues to stamp in my heart, it is the constant need to rely on him with a fresh heart each day. If you've seen the movie, *Elf,* you will recall how he went round and round through the revolving door, getting nowhere (Favreau, 2003).

I too have gone to God in similar fashion. I believe when there is a redundancy to my time of prayer and devotions, the "same ole same ole," I circle around and what use to be exciting becomes boring and mundane.

I have found that the changes God suggested (and I acted on) during my time in prayer, is how my relationship with Christ developed into something more beautiful and richer. I find joy praying God's agenda, not mine.

Starting each day with no change or expectation of God's presence often results in no time with God. It is a continual learning process to be purposeful to go each time through his open door, not a revolving door. It's not about conforming to the familiar, but embracing the unfamiliar.

The unpredictability of God is where I continue to find fullness of joy in him, where there is a constant flow and refreshing of his spirit.

"Aim at heaven and you will get earth thrown in. Aim at earth and you get neither" (Lewis, 1952, p. 135).

Conclusion

12

A Season for Everything

"A final word: Be strong in the Lord and in his mighty power...For we are not fighting against flesh-and-blood enemies, but against evil rulers and authorities of the unseen world, against mighty powers in this dark world, and against evil spirits in the heavenly places...Pray in the Spirit at all times and on every occasion. Stay alert and be persistent in your prayers for all believers everywhere" (Eph. 6:10–18, NLT).

What the world seeks in the supernatural as strange and unusual continues to attract attention. Television networks constantly air documentaries of experiences with mediums and other unseen, ungodly forces in the world. Many do not consider this fanatical, but intriguing.

People pray by lifting up their prayers to the universe, opposed to the maker of the universe. Things with God can also appear unusual, fanatical, and intriguing. Interestingly, when media and unbelievers hear from the Christian perspective about our supernatural God, they respond with doubt and a lack of interest, even hostility.

For those who read my experiences, they are unusual, but it is because God does not operate by human standards. He is mysterious, yet he is very generous and willing to share his being with all of us. He desires to make himself known to those who are willing.

The point of acknowledging God, who is supernatural, is to have a consciousness that all things are for him and for Christ to be lifted up, which in turn brings glory to the Father in heaven. I want the Holy Spirit to invade my entire being. I want my attention directed toward God first and foremost in all that I do. God wants my attention. God wants the world to know who he is and that he is God.

A steady dose of God developed a heightened sense of his presence in me. There is truly something marvelous that takes place when I'm willing to raise my hands to the heavens and submit to God.

By placing my body in a posture of humility, my faith increased and it's where God ushered me into his beautiful presence where I was completely submerged in him. It's how I am experiencing more of God's glory.

Experiencing the glory of God, for me has resulted in a greater awareness of his presence and his promises "on earth as it is in heaven." God wants me to look around and see his glory in everything. His beauty surrounds me and is meant to flow through me. I'm to be infused with the glory of God so others will see his beauty and want to share in the same. Share in the gift of salvation.

When the Israelites were freed from slavery they proclaimed, "Look, the Lord our God has shown us his glory and greatness, and we have heard his voice from the heart of the fire. Today we have seen that God can speak to us humans …" (Deut. 5:24, NLT). God still speaks through fire and often simply and gently to the heart and soul.

God wants me to recognize his greatness, how his glory fills the entire earth, and his glory is ever-present to speak and to guide, personally, step by step.

It is Christ, the glory of God, who willingly lavishes me with his presence. It's where I see clearly, regularly, and remarkably. What a delight it is to walk hand-in-hand with Christ. He is my faithful, loyal, friend.

This book was a difficult endeavor, primarily for the reasons stated in the beginning. Far too often I restrain from sharing the amazing things God has done (too much self-focus about what others may think).

God relentlessly put a desire in my heart saying, "The world needs hope, the world needs Jesus. How will they know? Take risks for Me. Use this book to boast in me and do not deviate from my message."

As I began to write this book, months passed until I admitted my struggle writing was because I wasn't writing God's story. I was writing what I thought others might be more comfortable with to avoid accusations of falsely sensationalizing the Gospel of Christ. Although, come to think of it, God *is* sensational! And the Gospel of Christ is illogical!

The more I obeyed God's directive, the more he demonstrated how truly sensational he is. He is spectacular in every way and I don't want to miss the *God-show*. There is nothing like it. There is no one like him. It stemmed from simple moments in God's presence. God took what was familiar and revealed how a little effort can bring about great miracles.

I've heard many sermons that challenge me to be a radical Christian. I allowed God to develop me so I can step out in bold ways that most Christians do not. In order to do this, I believe it begins by allowing God to radically express himself, his way.

God wants our full attention on him and him alone, and he is teaching me to be conscious of his presence and the many ways he reveals his righteousness. I had to ask myself, how will unbelievers come to know Christ if the conversation about the supernatural has been captured by the enemy as his exclusive domain? Was this another lie from the father of lies? Absolutely!

How will believers step up and be change-makers if they don't experience the fullness of God's glory? I don't believe we can be contagious Christians sticking to our safe, tidy routines, year after year, with no anticipation of God showing up.

"There are many who are so anxious to be led by some unseen power that they are ready to surrender the conduct of their lives to any spiritual or unseen person. In this way, they open their lives to the conduct and malevolent influence of evil spirits to the utter wreck and ruin of their lives" (Torrey, 1910).

Time in isolation led me to seeing things through God's viewpoint. Seeing God is where faith increases, and where discomfort is removed. Even in my smallest efforts, God lovingly and patiently guided me to move instinctively to his Word.

God kept reminding me not to limit him. "If my book helps only one person, it's worth it," I remind myself. These words were spoken over me when I wrote my first book and I found this an encouragement.

As I pressed on to complete this book, God convicted me that my goal should not be to impact a single person. God revealed that accepting—"if it helps one", dismissed his sovereignty. "I Am God", he spoke into my spirit. "I have promised I will accomplish infinitely more than you might ask or think" (Eph. 3:20).

He isn't just good, he is great, and wants his great and mighty works to be displayed so none will perish.

After my first book, I received blessings beyond what I thought would be possible. By God's grace and his mighty hand, he put my book into the hands of people I've never met and in multiple countries. In fact, it's been read by at least one person on every continent, excluding Antarctica. One day!

Since writing my first book, it's evident why God orchestrated this resource while living in Germany. The simplicity is how God is using it to reach people where English is a second language. I continue to marvel at how God puts his will in motion when we are obedient.

Whatever God asks me to do, every effort I attempt, with his help, I'll be successful (Prov. 16:3). God is too good and wonderful to settle for that which is not infinite.

I do not want to settle for "but one." He is an infinite God who will take what I do for him and harvest every seed he chooses and to whom he chooses. God doesn't play second-fiddle to anyone. God is sovereign, he's in control, and because I am his child, I don't have to settle for something small.

There was a time the book *Good to Great* was making its way through corporations. A message to be more than good—to achieve greatness. It's this mentality God has seared into my mind—he is a *great God*; he is *God Almighty!* He cannot be anything less. He is good, and what he does is great, always and forever.

God transformed my worship, so I could experience his unending grace in order to know him more. He taught me the importance of boasting in him and why I say I'm a Christian. I say I am a Christian in order to "reveal the righteousness of god in this world" (Lake, p. 458, 1994, emphasis mine).

Every day we face demands in our schedule. Whether they are for family or work. The result is we have less time for ourselves, let alone time for God. It is necessary to balance all things, but God must not be omitted from our busy, often overly scheduled day.

When God began challenging me to rethink how to worship, how it looks, he started with scripture, scripture called out for me to continually worship him, acknowledging his greatness, majesty, splendor, awe-inspiring deeds, including through signs and wonders.

Time with God nourishes my soul, day after day. Without question, I can wake up each day with hope, regardless of the situations and stresses of life. God is the constant that brings peace, comfort, unending love. Time with God is when I can confidently expect to see my invisible God. We have something the world does not have and that is peace and hope.

I cannot be a productive Christ follower without the commitment and intentionality to live a life with Jesus through worship and prayer. "But the secret of Christianity is not in doing. The secret is in being. Real Christianity is being a possessor of the nature of Jesus Christ" (Lake, 1994, p.7).

With human words, I can never adequately describe what it is to experience the weight of God's glory. You must experience him for yourself and keep your heart open for God to reveal his beauty in a variety of ways. I have a responsibility to give away my greatest secrets and my greatest joy, the Savior of the world, the presence of God who is within reach for all of us.

*"Be glad in your God. he's giving you a teacher to train you how
to live right—Teaching, like rain out of heaven, showers of words
to refresh and nourish your soul" (Joel 2:21–24, NLT).*

I do not want to hide God's goodness through a sense of silent humility. God does not want me to waste his goodness by keeping his wonders safely tucked away.

Another beautiful section of scripture to brag on God is this: "Don't let the wise brag of their wisdom. Don't let heroes brag of their exploits. Don't let the rich brag of their riches. If you brag, brag of this and this only: That you understand and know me. I'm God, and I act in loyal love. I do what's right and set things right and fair, and delight in those who do the same things. These are my trademarks, God's Decree" (Jer. 9:23, MSG).

The inward nourishment to my soul is to be an outward expression of his love. I want to carry an aroma of his substance. I want his Word rooted so deeply in me that everything I do will be traced back to his goodness, forgiveness, grace, and love.

*"To speak for God will be refreshing to ourselves,
cheering to saints, useful to sinners, and honoring to
the Savior" (Spurgeon, 2012, iTunes app).*

My daughter-in-law, Emma, posted on her Facebook status a beautiful way to focus on God each day:

"This morning I woke up in a nice warm bed. I have my health and so does my family. I had a hot cup of coffee while sitting on my couch, unafraid of contracting Ebola or being bombed. I was able to read my Bible and pray without fear of persecution. I drove to a job that pays a fair wage. Life can change in an instant. Today I'm going to be grateful."

This portrays a beautiful and simple way to recognize and share God's goodness in our lives and how we too can recognize and share the beauty of God's presence.

Though the world seems to be in chaos, with disease, financial crisis, human slavery, and wars on multiple continents, I know my ultimate security is in God alone.

Through a matrix of technology, I am confronted with the Word of God. I don't have to leave my house to be part of God's commission to learn and share the Good News of the cross. God wants me to stop my silence and Emma showed me a simple way to share the goodness of God. She saw God's glory around her and she shared his glory.

Learning to worship God without inhibition has become the gateway into God's presence. It is remarkable how effortless worship leads me to a deeper relationship with God. I can no longer be satisfied unless I sense God's continual, tangible presence.

The power of the Holy Spirit is what stirs the heart to perceive God's presence. "He is invisible, but he is real and perceptible" (Torrey, 1910).

My *Celestial Vision* gave a glimpse of how we can stroll with God, hand-in-hand, which brings tranquility and rest found in no other way. My prayer is for the accounts and experiences in this book to encourage and deepen your expectations of what God can and wants to do for and through you. Recognize your answered prayers are miracles and do not have to be a rarity. A praying believer opens up her soul to be filled and refreshed by the Holy Spirit.

Being in Christ and giving him full control of my being has been the most exhilarating cause for celebration through life's journey. My worship increased my love for God because he created me to worship him.

"God's various ministries are carried out everywhere; but they all originate in God's Spirit. God's various expressions of power are in action everywhere; but God himself is behind it all. Each person is given something to do that shows who God is: Everyone gets in on it, everyone benefits. All kinds of things are handed out by the Spirit, and to all kinds of people! The variety is wonderful: wise counsel, clear understanding, simple trust, healing the sick,

miraculous acts, proclamation distinguishing between spirits, tongues, interpretation of tongues. All these gifts have a common origin, but are handed out one by one by the one Spirit of God. He decides who gets what, and when" (1 Cor. 12:4–11, MSG).

At the end of this book I've provided several scripture passages describing the many ways God communicates. I will speak out, again and again, and boast in my God because there are no limits to who he is. I use these verses as a guide to worship, praise and thanks. They are my promises and my reality in walking with God.

God is enthroned above, majestic, worthy of all my praise and thanks. He is mighty in battle, invincible, to be honored for all he does and chooses to do. The acceptance of his love, freely given by the sacrifice on the cross and forgiveness of sins, is to live eternally with him because Life in him is Life itself. I can know him now so I can see him eternally. I want to walk with God and not just in a dream or vision.

Open your eyes to see as he sees. Let the Lord nourish you with an insatiable appetite for the spiritual, supernatural power of God. I have no doubt God's willingness to reveal himself comes from unrelenting prayers and an unquenchable urge to know him. Embrace the endless treasures of heaven.

I once heard a sermon how the virgin birth was scandalous grace. The birth of Christ was not done in the appropriate, respectful traditions, first in marriage and then conception. It was scandalous yet glorious. God is teaching me to have a heart that is willing to be scandalous for him and for the Truth of his Word!

It's been such a delight learning and experiencing how God can dominate my spirit without having to strive so hard to sense his presence. I continually ask myself, "What do I see today that shows how amazing my God is?" I don't want to become desensitized to his presence, power, and his glory. Jesus's first miracle turning water into wine, Mary told the disciples, "Do whatever he tells you" (John 2:5, NLT). May I do the same, just as Jesus says to, so I can experience my own miracles.

"God is not a secret to be kept." Remain humble, but not through silence. Get up, shout out, and applaud God for all he is and does. The Lord captured my heart in an entirely new way. "His greatness is beyond discovery, but all have the privilege to discover him!" (Matt. 5:14–16, MSG).

God's story is simple. He is holy, we are not. He wants us to be with him forever, so he paid for our sins himself. Jesus died on the cross for all nations. He rose to life and lives today. He sits at the right hand of God the Father, intercedes on my behalf, and on your behalf. He gives me God-stories to share of his goodness, grace, forgiveness, and love.

How can you be a God-connector to reveal to the world the love and saving grace of Jesus Christ? The greatness of God Almighty! What's your God-story?

References

Adema, R. (2000). "Apple of God's Eye." Birmingham: Doctoral Studies Bible Church. File D100119. Retrieved from http://www.doctrinalstudies.com/pdf/D100119.pdf [Accessed: November 18, 2014].

Addison, D. (2013). *Night Dreams Reveal Your Life Dream.* Santa Maria: InLight Connection.

Beal, V. (2014). "The Difference between a Computer Virus, Worm, and Trojan Horse." City: Webopedia: QuinStreet Enterprises. Retrieved from http://www.webopedia.com/DidYouKnow/Internet/2004/virus.asp. [Accessed: October 29, 2013].

Bittner, J. (2013). *Breaking the Veil of Silence.* Reston: TOS Publishing.

Bounds, E.M. and Murray, A. (2003). *E.M. Bounds and Andrew Murray on Prayer.* Grand Rapids: TimelessReads.com. iTunes e-book.

Bounds, E. M. (2000). *The Complete Works of E.M. Bounds on Prayer.*

Grand Rapids: Baker Books.

Bounds, E. M. (n.d.). *Prayer Miracles.* City: Publisher. Chapter 13. Retrieved online: http://www.worldinvisible.com/library/bounds/5bb.10597-possibilities/5bb.10597.13.htm. [Accessed: October 1, 2014].

Churchill, W. (n.d.) Sir Winston Churchill, British Statesman, Prime Minister, http://www.values.com/inspirational-quotes/6650-to-each-there-comes-in-their-lifetime-a-special. [Accessed: November 4, 2016].

Clark, R. (2011). *The Essential Guide to healing.* Bloomington: Chosen Books. iBooks file.

Dictionary.com. *Breath* in Dictionary.com Unabridged. Source location: Random House, Inc. http://dictionary.reference.com/browse/skill. Available: http://dictionary.reference.com/. [Accessed: May 31, 2015].

Dictionary.com. *Enjoy* in Dictionary.com Unabridged. Source location: Random House, Inc. http://dictionary.reference.com/browse/skill. Available: http://dictionary.reference.com/. [Accessed: May 4, 2015].

Dictionary.com. *Indisputable* in Dictionary.com Unabridged. Source location: Random House, Inc. http://dictionary.reference.com/browse/skill. Available: http://dictionary.reference.com/. [Accessed: May 20, 2015].

Dictionary.com. *Mercy* in Dictionary.com Unabridged. Source location: Random House, Inc. http://dictionary.reference.com/browse/skill. Available: http://dictionary.reference.com/. [Accessed: May 20, 2015].

Dictionary.com. *Miracle* in Dictionary.com Unabridged. Source location: Random House, Inc. http://dictionary.reference.com/browse/skill. Available: http://dictionary.reference.com/. [Accessed: May 31, 2015].

Dictionary.com. *Organic* in Dictionary.com Unabridged. Source location: Random House, Inc. http://dictionary.reference.com/

browse/skill. Available: http://dictionary.reference.com/. [Accessed: June 14, 2014].

Dictionary.com. *Presence* in Dictionary.com Unabridged. Source location: Random House, Inc. http://dictionary.reference.com/browse/skill. Available: http://dictionary.reference.com/. [Accessed: May 31, 2015].

Dictionary.com. *Supernatural* in Dictionary.com Unabridged. Source location: Random House, Inc. http://dictionary.reference.com/browse/skill. Available: http://dictionary.reference.com/. [Accessed: May 4, 2015].

Dictionary.com. *Upon* in Dictionary.com Unabridged. Source location: Random House, Inc. http://dictionary.reference.com/browse/skill. Available: http://dictionary.reference.com/. [Accessed: May 31, 2015].

Elf. (2003). [DVD] Los Angeles: Rhythm & Hues Studios.

Gladwell, M. (2000). *The Tipping Point: How Little Things Can Make a Big Difference.* New York: Little, Brown and Company.

Goll, J. and Goll, M. (2006). *Dream Language: The Prophetic Power of Dreams, Revelations, and the Spirit of Wisdom.* Shippensburg, PA. Destiny Image Publishing, Inc.

Henry, M. (1706). "Matthew henry's Concise Commentary." Christian Notes. Retrieved from http://www.christnotes.org/commentary.php?b=66&c=1&com=mhc. [Accessed: October 14, 2013].

Houghton, I., Massey, M. (2012). "Your Presence is heaven." [online] YouTube. Available at: https://www.youtube.com/watch?v=yNAvRdSkE10 [Accessed: November 18, 2014].

Ibojie, J. (2005). *Illustrated Dictionary of Dream Symbols.* Pescara, Italy: Destiny Image Europe srl. iBook file.

Johnson, B. (2012). *Hosting the Presence: Unveiling heaven's Agenda.* Shippensburg: Destiny Image Publishers, Inc.

Kinlaw, D.F. (2002). *This Day with the Master.* Grand Rapids: Zondervan.

Lake, J. (1994). *John G. Lake: his Life, his Sermons, his Boldness of Faith.* Fort Worth: Kenneth Copeland Publications.

Lawrence, Bro. (2008). *The Practice of the Presence of God: The Best Rule of a Holy Life.* Radford: Wilder Publications. Kindle e-book.

Lewis, C. S. (1952). *Mere Christianity.* New York: HarperCollins Publishers.

Life Application Study Bible (1988). New Living Translation. Wheaton: Tenderly House Publishing, Inc.

Lowry, H. (1876). Nothing but the Blood. [online] Hymnary. Available at: http://www.hymnary.org/text/what_can_wash_away_my_sin. [Accessed: March 26, 2015].

Murray, A. (1953). *The Master's Indwelling.* Radford: Wilder Publications. (1895). iBook file.

Murray, A. (1898). *The Ministry of Intercession.* London: James Nisbet & Co., Ltd. 3rd Edition. (1917). iBook file.

Names of God Bible. (2013). Biblegateway.com. Retrieved Online: http://www.biblegateway.com/passage/?search=Luke%20 19:37-40&version=NOG [Accessed: November 13, 2013].

Orton, D. (2002). "An Open Heaven." Retrieved online: http://chosenoneministries.com/articles/an_open_heaven.htm. Mt Eliza VIC, Australia. www.lifemessenger.org. [Accessed: August 27, 2014].

Sheikh, B. and Schneider, R. H. (1978). *I Dared to Call Him Father.* Grand Rapids: Chosen Books.

Simpson, A. B. (1897). *Days of heaven Upon Earth.* Brooklyn: Christian Alliance Publishing Co.

Sligh, C. (2008). *Empty Me.* [CD] Santa Monica: Universal Music Publishing Group.

Sparks, T.A. (2011) *Spiritual Senses.* Abbotsford: Life Sentence Publishing, LLC.

Sparks, T.A. (1973). *Prophetic Ministry.* Forest Hill, London: "Witness and Testimony Literature Trust" Magazine. iTunes e-book.

Sparks, T. A. (2012). Spiritual Sight. Forest Hill, London: Original Version: "A Witness and A Testimony" magazines (9942-1944). Vols. 20-5 through 22-1. http://www.austin-sparks.net/english/books/spiritual_sight.html. iTunes e-book.

Spurgeon, C. (2012). *The Surgeon Morning and Evening.* iTunes app.

Spurgeon, C. (n.d.) *The Son Glorified by the Father and the Father Glorified by the Son.* Metropolitan Tabernacle Pulpit 1. Volume 25, NO. 1465A. London: METROPOLITAN TABERNACLE. Retrieved online: http://www.spurgeongems.org/vols25-27/chs1465A.pdf [Accessed: October 9, 2014].

"Tip the scales." Cambridge Dictionary of American Idioms. (2006). Cambridge University Press 8 Feb. 2016 http://idioms.thefreedictionary.com/tip+the+scales. [Accessed: May 4, 2015].

Torrey, R. A. (1910). *The Person and Work of the Holy Spirit.* London and Edinburgh. iTunes e-book. (1974).

Tozer, A. W. (2009). *The Pursuit of God.* Easford. Martino Fine Books. (1948).

Tozer, A. W. (2003). *The Attributes of God.* Volume I. Camp Hill: Wing Spread Publishers. (1997).

Tozer, A. W. (2014). [online] oChristian.com. Ontario: ChristiansUnite. Retrieved from http://christian-quotes.ochristian.com/The-Trinity-Quotes/. [Accessed: September 25, 2014].

Vallotton, K. (2007). *Developing a Supernatural Lifestyle.* Shippensburg: Destiny Image Publisher, Inc.

Wilkerson, D. (2014). *It's Time to Close the Door.* Melbourne: Publisher. Retrieved online: http://davidwilkersontoday.blogspot.de/2014/10/its-time-to-close-door.html. [Accessed: October 14, 2014].

Williams, D. (2013). *We the People: Presidential Quotations and Milestone Documents.* Carson City: http://www.todayinsci.com/K/Kennedy_John/KennedyJohn-Quotations.htm. [Accessed: March 25, 2015].

Reagan, W. & United Pursuit. (2013). Live at the Banks House. [DVD] Knoxville: United Pursuit Records.

God Speaks Again and Again

Take a moment to evaluate the variety of ways you have been engaged in conversation with God. Desire more and expect God to reveal himself, not just in ways you understand, but in the mysterious ways of his unlimited resources and creativity. Submerge yourself into God's presence and listen for his voice.

- *Angels.* Gen. 16" "The angel added." "The angel said. "The angel told." Gen. 19: two angels arrived. Num. 22:25: "when the donkey saw the angel of the Lord …" A donkey sees an angel …" This donkey was smarter and wiser than most humans. Matt. 17:5: But even as he spoke, a bright cloud overshadowed them, and a voice from the cloud said "This is my dearly loved Son, who brings me great joy. Listen to him." God spoke through an angel.
- *Apostles.* Eph. 4:11: "He handed out gifts of apostle, prophet, evangelists, and pastor, teacher to train Christ's followers."
- *Church.* Num. 7:89: "Whenever Moses went into the Tabernacle to speak with the Lord, he heard the voice speaking to him."
- *Cloud.* Num. 11:25: "And the Lord came down in the cloud and spoke to Moses …"
- *Dreams.* Gen. 28:12; Gen. 31:10; Dan. 1:17
- *Dry Seasons of Life/Wilderness.* Num. 9:1: "… A *year* after Israel's departure from Egypt, the Lord spoke to Moses in the wilderness of Sinai. [emphasis mine 2016]

- *Evangelist.* Eph. 4:11: "He handed out gifts of apostle, prophet, evangelist, and pastor-teacher to train Christ's followers." Acts 2:8: "Philip the evangelist …"
- *Faithful Promises.* Num. 23:19: "God is not a man, so he does not lie. He is not human, so he does not change his mind. Has he ever spoken and failed to act? Has he ever promised and not carried it through?"
- *Fire.* Deut. 5:4, 10:4: "… the Lord had spoken from the heart of the fire …"
- *From heaven.* Ex. 6:28: "… spoke to you from heaven …"
- *Giving Orders.* Ex. 6:13: "But the Lord spoke to Moses and Aaron and gave them orders …"
- *Holy Spirit.* Luke 2:26: "revealed by the Holy Spirit" Jn. 14:17: "He is the Holy Spirit, who leads into all truth. The world cannot receive him, because it isn't looking for him and doesn't recognize him …"
- *Immediately.* Mt. 14:27: "But Jesus spoke to them at once …"
- *In his Presence.* Gen. 19:27: "Abraham got up early that morning and hurried out to the place where he had stood in the Lord's presence." Ex. 34:29: "When Moses came down Mount Sinai carrying the two stone tablets inscribed with the terms of the covenant, he wasn't aware that his face had become radiant because he had spoken to the Lord."
- *Instructions.* 2 Kings 22:15: "The Lord, the God of Israel, has spoken! Go back and tell the man who sent you …" Isa. 28:26: "God instructs"
- *In the Night.* Gen. 46:2: "during the night God spoke"
- *In the storm.* Job 38:1: "… God answered Job from the eye of a violent storm." Psalm 104:4: "The winds are your messengers …"
- *Loud voice.* Deut. 5:22: "He spoke with a loud voice …"
- *Man (pastors, teachers, friends, etc.).* Deut. 5:5: "I stood as an intermediary between you and the Lord … he spoke to me, and I passed his words on to you." Num. 12:2: "They

said, 'Has the Lord spoken only through Moses? Hasn't he spoken through us, too?'"

- *Mountains.* Isa. 55:12: "… The mountains and hills will burst into song."
- *Parables, riddles, and figures of speech.* Jn. 16:25: "I have spoken of these matters in figures of speech, but soon I will stop speaking figuratively and will tell you plainly all about the Father." Mat. 13:34: Jesus used stories and illustrations. Also, see Dreams.
- *Pastors.* Eph. 4:11: "he handed out gifts of apostle, prophet, evangelist, and pastor-teacher to train Christ's followers."
- *Personally.* 2 Sam. 23:3: "The God of Israel spoke … said *to me …*"
- *Prophets.* I Cor. 12:28: "And God has placed in the church first of all apostles, second prophets …" Eph. 4:11–12: "… gifts Christ gave to the church: the apostles, the prophets. Their responsibility is to equip God's people to do his work and build up the church, the body of Christ."
- *Seers.* 1 Chr. 29:29: "All the events of King David's reign, from beginning to end, are written in The Record of Samuel Seer, The Record of Nathan the Prophet, and The Record of Gad the Seer."
- *Silence.* Gen. 1:1–3: "From the void, God speaks, 'Let there be light.'"
- *Spirit and Life.* Jn. 6:63 "The Spirit alone gives eternal life… words I have spoken to you are spirit and life."
- *Stillness.* Ex. 14:13: "… stand still and watch the Lord rescue you today." Psalm 46:10: "Be still, and know that I am God!"
- *Stones.* Deut. 5:22: "… and he wrote his words on two stone tablets and gave them to me …"
- *Teachers.* Eph. 4:11: "he handed out gifts of apostle, prophet, evangelist, and pastor-teacher to train Christ's followers." Acts 23:9: "Now in the church … were prophets and teachers."
- *The Word is God.* Jn. 1

- *Thunder.* 1 Sam. 7:10 "… the Lord spoke with a mighty voice of thunder from heaven …"
- *Times of offering and sacrifice.* Num. 7:89: "he heard the Voice speaking to him from between the two angel-cherubim above the Atonement-Cover on the Chest of The Testimony. He spoke with him."
- *Touch of his Hand.* Deut. 9:10: "The Lord gave me the two tablets on which God had written with his own finger all the words he had spoken …"
- *Trance.* Acts 10:10; Acts 11:5; and Acts 22:17: "I was praying (Peter) in the city of Joppa when I fell into a trance."
- *Visions.* Gen. 15:1: "… the Lord spoke to Abram in a vision …" Gen. 46:2: "During the night God spoke to him in a vision …"
- *Voice.* Deut. 4:12: "… there was only a voice."
- *Warning.* Deut. 4:15: "But be very careful! You did not see the Lord's form on the day he spoke to you …"
- *Wherever You Are, Wherever You Go.* Prov. 15:3: "The Lord is watching everywhere …" Jer. 23:24: "… Am I not everywhere in all the heavens and earth?"
- *Whisper.* 1 Kings 19:11–12: but God wasn't to be found in the wind; God wasn't in the earthquake; not in the fire; but through a whisper. Job 4:12-16: "A word came to me in secret—a mere whisper of a word, but I heard it clearly."
- *Word of Knowledge.* 1 Cor. 12:8: "…Spirit gives a message of special knowledge."

"I've preached you to the whole congregation,
I've kept back nothing, God—you know that.
I didn't keep the news of your ways
a secret, didn't keep it to myself.
I told it all, how dependable you are, how thorough.
I didn't hold back pieces of love and truth
For myself alone. I told it all,
let the congregation know the whole story (Ps. 40:9–10).

Additional Reading by Teresa

Blog: www.teresaodden.com
Facebook: https://www.facebook.com/teresaodden.blog.gmail/
Twitter: https://twitter.com/tlodden01

Beautiful Dreamer: Dreams—God's Personal Navigation System is a book that reveals the glory of God. God took two dreams over the course of a year and gently guided Teresa on an unexpected journey. A journey that took her from the corporate world of America to the Black Forest of Germany. Get your e-book on Amazon. Printed copies also available.

Customer Reviews and Comments:

- "An amazing faith building book."
- "Challenging and inspiring."
- "Power of dreams and journaling."
- "Could not put it down. You have helped to reawaken my strong belief in God's guiding hand."
- "This book speaks straight to the heart and very inspirational. Thank you for inviting the world into your life. I hope I can open my heart for others one day."
- "I never paid attention to my dreams until I read your book. I started praying and asking God to speak to me through dreams and he is."
- "My English isn't very good. Your stories of God's love was easy to understand."

Beautiful Dreamer

Dreams—God's Personal
Navigation System

Part 1

Resort Dream

*"For God speaks again and again, though people do
not recognize it. He speaks in dreams, in visions of
the night, when deep sleep falls on people as they lie
in their beds. He whispers in their ears and terrifies
them with warnings" (Job 33:14–16, LASB).*

I call this my *resort dream*. It was the first of two dreams given to me
as preparation for a time when my world would turn "upside down."
Little by little, over the course of a year, the meaning became clear.
"God speaks again and again, yet people don't recognize it.

Resort Dream

*I was in a resort with my husband and two sons. It was the kind of
resort that includes a casino. We were in the lobby, and I was in a white
robe having just returned from the spa. I told my husband I wanted
another spa treatment, and he encouraged me to do so. I looked up to
my right at the board listing all the spa options. "I want that one," I
exclaimed with a thrill, "to be bathed and soaked in the finest of oils," as
I pointed to the top of the list. "Okay," my husband said, supporting and
affirming my desires, and off he went with our boys.*

*I proceeded to go by way of the elevator, which was to my left. The
lobby became crowded because the casino was opening. I looked up to my
right and saw my husband and sons on the upper deck preparing to scout
out the hotel. As I was making my way through the crowd, a young boy,
maybe twelve, was passing out one-dollar coins. I took my coin and saw
a slot machine ahead. The slot machine was a box decorated with gold
glitter. I worked my way through the crowd, and it seemed that all eyes
were on me. The crowd began to surround me the closer I got to the box.
As my arm was outstretched, preparing to insert the coin, I said to myself,
"I'm going to win." As the coin dropped through the slot, the box lit up
and started shaking, announcing that I had won $1,000. I had no doubt
I was going to win.*

I heard shouts from the crowd that the money belonged to the boy. I said, "No, I won it, and it's mine." The crowd continued to yell that it was the boy's. A man from my church, who was a board member, and his wife stared at me in silence. They were not coming to my defense, and, I sensed they, too, felt the same as the crowd, that I should give the boy my winnings. In that moment I stood alone feeling as though everyone was against me and judging me. "That boy was giving away coins, as though he was throwing them in the trash. I chose to do something with mine." I told the crowd, and I turned confidently to leave.

When I spun around to leave, a life-sized drawing appeared. It was a vision within my dream. There was no artist, just the drawing, which began sketching the back of three men standing in a row side-by-side. The sketch was in black pencil, but there was no visible canvas. The drawing got faster and faster, and their backs became peacock feathers. As the drawing picked up speed, the picture became distorted, and all the beautiful feathers were now one big, black blob. When the scribbling stopped, the man in the middle stepped out of the drawing, turned around to face me, and became a live person. When he faced me, his legs were rooted in the ground as though he was a tree. he had black hair done in cornrows, and worms were embedded throughout his hair all the way down to the roots. I was disgusted. I was about to run away, but I turned back, still in my white robe, and asked, "What do the worms mean?"

"Listen to me," was all he said.

I quickly turned to run away, but I turned back and again asked, "What do the worms mean?"

"Listen to me," he said again.

The third time I went to run away, I turned back and asked again, "What do the worms mean?"

"I am a prophet; listen to me," were the final words he said to me.

End of dream—January 12, 2011

Biblical Concepts I Discovered about Dreams

It is the Holy Spirit who guides us into all truth (John 14:12–17).

Prayer is the key to revealing things unknown (2 Sam. 7:27).

Ask the Holy Spirit to speak to my spirit when my body and mind are physically at rest (Job 33:14–16).

Keep my eyes open for the ways that God may be speaking to me as he uses different means to speak to different people (1 Cor. 12:6 and Job 33:14–16).

Dreams and visions are often strategies for interceding on behalf of people and situations, but they can also be to warn, redirect, and keep us from pride (Job 33:14–16, Dan. 6:10, and Luke 2:37).

Keep a journal to record my spiritual journey: record prayers, requests, and encouraging and thoughtful words from others, as well as dreams and visions (Num. 33:2, Isa. 8:16, and Jer. 30:2).

Dreams are similar to a movie trailer giving the key features of things to come. Seek God to understand the complete picture (Ps. 78:1–2 and John 16:13).

Through prayer God prepares and through dreams God awakens to see as he sees (Ps. 111:3, Dan. 2:19–23, Job 4:12, 13, Isa. 48:6, and 1 Cor. 2:9–13).

Be patient and trust the Lord one step at a time (Ps. 32:8, Ps. 37:23, and Prov. 3:5–6).

I don't have to think I know what God said through prayer, the reading of his Word, and time in his presence, I can know and make decisions based on this certainty (Ps. 57:7, John 10:27, and James 1:5–8).

A "little" of God will not move the hand of God (Matt. 26:36–45, John 14:10–14, 1 Tim. 4:14–16, and 2 Pet. 1:16–20).

Walking by sight leaves little room for miracles (2 Cor. 5:7, Ps. 77:14).

God is willing to surprise me at daybreak allowing me to rest in him so he will confirm the work that he wants me to do (Ps. 90: 12–17, Ps. 143:7–10, Eph. 2:8–9).

About the Author

After twenty-one years in philanthropy at one of the largest foundations in the world, God redirected Teresa, and she moved to Europe with her husband Rick. She dropped her two sons off at college, relocated to Germany, and it was there she wrote her first book, *Beautiful Dreamer: Dreams—God's Personal Navigation System*, and became a blogger (teresaodden.com). Teresa didn't set out to be an author/writer, but God had different plans. The verse, "I can do all things through Christ who strengthens me," took on a whole new meaning for her. God challenged her to experience more of his glory so that others will see him in the fullness of his glory. The more she experiences God, she has a passion to see others walk in the supernatural power of God. Her ministry includes revealing God's creativity through dreams and visions. Teresa has been married for thirty-two years, both sons are married, all serving the Lord, and three grandchildren (Rose Marie, Margaux, and Elijah). She loves time with family and friends and mentoring young women. Travel is at the top of her list for adventure, primarily to warmer climates—with Spain and Croatia at the top of her list. Teresa is a dreamer, a God-dreamer.

CPSIA information can be obtained
at www.ICGtesting.com
Printed in the USA
BVHW02s2036130518
515782BV00016B/142/P